Living Happier After

LIVING Happier AFTER

20 Women Talk About Life After Divorce

WILMA JONES

Dedication

To the memory of Walter "Howard" McCree, Jr.

Disclaimer
This book is written for informational and entertainment purposes. Neither the author nor the publisher of this book is in the business of providing relationship, legal, financial or other professional services or advice. As such, neither the author nor the publisher can be liable for your actions due to reading this book. You should contact competent professional advisors before making decisions about what is best for you. The author and publisher specifically disclaim any personal liability, loss or risk incurred as a consequence of the use and application, either directly or indirectly, of any information presented herein. Any similarity of fictional persons in this book to actual persons living or dead is purely coincidental.

Portions of this book first appeared on the author's website.
The author gratefully acknowledges the individuals who have contributed their stories, thoughts and recollections to this project.

Copyright © 2012 by Wilma Jones. All rights reserved.

ISBN: 0692459545
ISBN 13: 9780692459546

No part of this publication may be reproduced, stored in a retrieval system, or transmitted, in any form or by any means, electronic, mechanical, photocopying, recording or otherwise, without the prior permission of the publishers.

Table of Contents

Foreword · xiii
Introduction · xvii
Chapter 1 The Strategies ·1
Chapter 2 Managing Your Thoughts · · · · · · · · · · · · · · · ·7
  Adrienne – Something So Simple · · · · · · · · · · · · · ·8
  Vicki – Looking For an Upgrade · · · · · · · · · · · · · ·12
  Cynthia – It Wasn't Even About Me · · · · · · · · · · · ·16
  Camille – I Love You · 19
  Melissa – Dad Never Says Nasty Things · · · · · · · · · ·21
  Teresa – All about Me ·24
  Lisa – Run It Out ·26
  Tamra – Fit the Mold ·29
  Sheree – Break That Mold · · · · · · · · · · · · · · · · · ·31
  Peggy – Owe It to Essence · · · · · · · · · · · · · · · · · ·32
  Danielle – Nothing to Compare · · · · · · · · · · · · · · ·34
  Kathy – Life Is Too Short · · · · · · · · · · · · · · · · · · ·37
  Kim – There Is Life After · · · · · · · · · · · · · · · · · · ·39
  Alexis – The Freedom of Lifting · · · · · · · · · · · · · · ·41
  Taylor – What You Create · · · · · · · · · · · · · · · · · · 42
  Kandi – Worth a Lot · 44
  Gretchen – Surround Myself with Positive · · · · · · · · · 46
  Jacqueline – We Just Outgrew One Another · · · · · · · · 48
  Caroline – A Real Spoiled Brat · · · · · · · · · · · · · · · ·51
  Dina – The Forgiveness Factor · · · · · · · · · · · · · · · ·54

Chapter 3 Doing Good for Others · · · · · · · · · · · · · · ·59
   Alexis – Shines From Within · · · · · · · · · · · · 60
   Kim – Assisting and Supporting · · · · · · · · · · · ·61
   Kandi – Unconditionally · · · · · · · · · · · · · · · · ·62
   Tamra – Be of Service · · · · · · · · · · · · · · · · 63
   Sheree – Fostering ·65
   Cynthia – Book Club · · · · · · · · · · · · · · · · · 66
   Dina – Kept the Name · · · · · · · · · · · · · · · · ·67
   Adrienne – What Single Women Do · · · · · · · · · ·69
   Camille – He's My Son · · · · · · · · · · · · · · · · ·71
   Melissa – Little Things · · · · · · · · · · · · · · · · · ·73
   Kathy – Good with My Dogs · · · · · · · · · · · · · ·75
   Teresa – An Unlikely Friend · · · · · · · · · · · · · ·77
   Peggy – Once I Had Something to Say · · · · · · · · ·79
Chapter 4 Nurturing Relationships · · · · · · · · · · · · · · ·81
   Kandi – Forgiving the Abuse · · · · · · · · · · · · · ·82
   Kathy – Daily Conversations with God · · · · · · · · ·85
   Peggy – He Was a Lost Soul · · · · · · · · · · · · · ·87
   Teresa – Forgive and Move On · · · · · · · · · · · · ·89
   Melissa – Forgive Me and Him · · · · · · · · · · · · ·91
   Alexis – He's Moved On · · · · · · · · · · · · · · · · ·94
   Sheree – My Kids Forgiveness · · · · · · · · · · · · ·95
   Tamra – Forgiveness Is Not Needed · · · · · · · · · ·97
   Vicki – My Relationship with My Parents · · · · · · · · · 99
   Dina – It was My Mom · · · · · · · · · · · · · · · · ·103
   Lisa – Nurtured My Son · · · · · · · · · · · · · · · ·105
   Caroline – Release ·107
   Camille – Nurtured My Kids · · · · · · · · · · · · · ·108
   Adrienne – She Got Me Outta that Funk · · · · · · · ·109
   Cynthia – My Friends and the Word · · · · · · · · · ·111
   Gretchen – Spiritual Experience · · · · · · · · · · · · ·112

Chapter 5   Engaging in Activities · · · · · · · · · · · · · · · · · · · 113
   Kandi – Everybody Ain't Your Friend · · · · · · · · · · · · · 114
   Dina – My Cheerleaders · 116
   Tamra – Sex · 117
   Cynthia – What I Want To Do · · · · · · · · · · · · · · · · · · · 119
   Caroline – I Do That · 121
   Teresa – Joy · 122
   Vicki – Laser Focused · 123
   Lisa – Music · 125
   Alexis – Enjoy Me · 126
   Kathy – I Make It Happen · 127
   Melissa – The Club Rub · 129
   Adrienne – Release Boundaries · · · · · · · · · · · · · · · · · 131
   Kim – In The Game · 132
   Peggy – Control · 133
   Sheree – All Along · 135
Chapter 6   Gratitude · 137
   Camille – Forever Grateful · 138
   Lisa – A Real Friend · 141
   Cynthia – My Way · 143
   Vicki – For That Season · 146
   Teresa – Karma · 149
   Dina – Forgiven · 151
   Caroline – Three Things · 152
   Tamra – A Good Steward · 153
   Sheree – Life and Love · 154
   Kim – Learning · 155
   Kathy – A Home · 156
   Adrienne – Starting Over · 157
   Alexis – Independence · 158
   Melissa – Two Things · 159

Peggy – Healthy and Wise · · · · · · · · · · · · · · · · · · · 162
Jacqueline – A Positive Spin · · · · · · · · · · · · · · · · 163
Danielle – My Children · 164
Chapter 7 Living in the Moment · · · · · · · · · · · · · · · · 167
Lisa – No Regrets · 168
Alexis – Listen · 169
Adrienne – Therapy · 170
Cynthia – Moment · 171
Gretchen – Not Perfect · 173
Kim – Let No One Disrupt · · · · · · · · · · · · · · · · · 175
Sheree – Balance Sheet · · · · · · · · · · · · · · · · · · · 176
Melissa – A Little Bit Everyday · · · · · · · · · · · · · · 177
Tamra – I Do What is In Front of Me · · · · · · · · · 178
Peggy – You're Going to Have It · · · · · · · · · · · · 180
Teresa – Not the Avenger · · · · · · · · · · · · · · · · · 182
Camille – No Rentals · 184
Vicki – About You · 186
Caroline – One Minute · 187
Kathy – Seconds and Frames · · · · · · · · · · · · · · 188
Dina – Do Today · 189
Chapter 8 Time for Yourself · · · · · · · · · · · · · · · · · · · 191
Caroline – Be the Best Person · · · · · · · · · · · · · 192
Gretchen – I Know Where I Fit · · · · · · · · · · · · · 193
Peggy – Learning to Say No · · · · · · · · · · · · · · · 195
Alexis – Sundays · 196
Lisa – Baths · 197
Adrienne – Back To School · · · · · · · · · · · · · · · 198
Kim – De-Program · 199
Camille – Find the Time to Love You · · · · · · · · 200
Melissa – Taking the Time to Think · · · · · · · · · ·202
Cynthia – What a Treasure · · · · · · · · · · · · · · · · 204
Kathy – Precious ·206

Sheree – Peace ·207
Vicki – Don't Waste It · 208
Chapter 9 The Survey ·209
            Acknowledgements ·227

Foreword

Life happens quickly. And when you have a relationship ending, it can be most unsettling for your world.

Divorcing someone can be the most earth-shattering experience you can have. It leaves you feeling raw with pain, full of shame and with a sagging ego.

But there is life after divorce, sometimes an even better life. You can still live your life with joy as suggested by Wilma Jones, author of *Living Happier After*. It's really true! But you must embrace your emotions and release the past memories. After all, pain is just life happening.

A friend of mine contacted me one day a few months after her divorce and asked, "Is there such a thing as 'good pain'?" I began to think about that question in many ways. This is what I know about loss and relationships. Nothing stays the same. All things evolve over time. And what can seem like an end is almost always a new beginning. It's when you're going through the turmoil, pain, and sorrow that this awareness escapes you. That's why a book on the subject of getting beyond your divorce grief is so essential.

I remember getting a call from a dear friend at 1:00 a.m. screaming and crying in pain and wanting immediate relief. I threw on some clothes and rushed to her side. Her divorce had been finalized that same day and the reality of her loss was now registering big time.

When she opened her door, she looked like she had been on a battlefield. We sat and talked about what was really occurring right now. Where there's no pain, there's no gain. My friend was giving emotional birth to herself and what she was experiencing was labor pain. Little did she know that an entire new experience was about to take her life by storm.

I told her that she was now heading for what I labeled as "post divorce bliss." That means that her life was shifting and making room for new experiences. But let me back up for a moment and address the emotional process of ending a marriage.

When a relationship ends, we go through a process much like a slow death, which includes many stages. The first stage is a feeling of disbelief—you can't believe it's happening to you. The second stage is—how can he do this to me! In the third stage, you bargain. You'll do anything to keep things intact. And after the stunning recognition of the reality, you reach the fourth stage, which is you grapple with the truth—it's over.

When you face loss that is the point in which your grief is most intense. You may stay in bed for days. You have crazy thoughts like, "it was all my fault." You can't imagine life going on. But just remember, it takes two to make a relationship last and two to take it apart.

Getting help will allow you to come to that realization. You will shut down for a while, then regroup. Then it will occur to you that your relationship died, not you.

In order to move ahead and meet the future, you'll need to create a new definition of the person from whom you have separated. You can also do this by 1) letting go of the bitterness and shame, 2) giving up the need for revenge, 3) stop obsessing about the injury and reengage with life, 4) redefine the other person's behavior in terms of his own personal struggles, and 5) replace blame and

Foreword

shame with empathy. If you find it difficult to forgive and let go, seek counseling or a support group.

Finally, identify a mentor—someone who you look up to and wish to imitate. Then adopt the traits of your mentor that you want to incorporate into your new persona. You're now ready to tackle the following:

Healing

- Healthy diet
- Healthy spirit
- Healthy heart
- Healthy life purpose

At this point, you're ready to do what I call re-mothering. Re-mothering:

- Care for self
- Support of self
- Affirmation of worth
- Loving gestures
- Giving honor through consistency

Since wives initiate at least 65 percent of divorces, they need a guidebook like *Living Happier After*. When Wilma asked me to explore this topic—divorce—I agreed without hesitation because I know giving women voices to express their journey can be so empowering for them.

Once again, divorce is not an ending; it's a whole new beginning. It's living your life with a new focus. It's finding new friends and establishing new intellectual and social experiences. And finally, it's figuring out that you are responsible for your own life and joy.

Having done these steps, you're on the road past divorce to living a happier life.

Audrey B. Chapman
Therapist, Author of *Getting Good Loving: How to Find and Make Love Last*, and Talk Show host of The Audrey Chapman Show (WHUR-FM and H.U.R. Voices on Sirius XM Satellite Channel 141)

Introduction

I'll never forget the moment I realized I was going to have to get a divorce. I was sitting at my desk in our home office loading tracking software onto my laptop. It had sunk to this level. Yes, I was about to use technology to track the whereabouts of my husband's car! I thought to myself, this wasn't the person I wanted to become when I was a little girl.

My true, genuine self never pictured herself having to fight so damn hard to keep her marriage together. Then I realized, I never even expected to get married. I was always the super-smart, super-loud, extremely tall girl who always had a boyfriend, but never kept him long. Once they cheated, lied or hurt me, I kicked them to the curb, determining that they were no prize. 'Cause I was always looking for the prize in life. I felt I was special and the person I was supposed to be with, if there was just *one*, had to be, too.

As I watched the laptop screen denote the progress of the installation I suddenly hit 'cancel.' I knew at that moment that my husband was no longer a prize to me anymore. And obviously since his behavior was hurtful and disrespectful to me, I wasn't a prize to him anymore either. It no longer made sense to fight for someone who really didn't want to treat me the way I needed to be treated. It was clear that this wasn't working anymore.

While loading the software that afternoon, I came to the understanding with myself that I had to stop trying to make this thing work all alone. I felt as if my spouse would let us down and disappoint the family often. Nagging and lying, lying and nagging, that was what we were about. Our children heard the arguments and saw me cry. I think they knew it was coming, too, but we would tell them, 'No, we're never getting divorced.' Until the day, we said that we were.

I had hoped to have a reasonable divorce. No drama, no lawyers, no judges making decisions for us about our family. That was a joke. Why I thought the lies and deception would cease because we were separated, I do not know. It seemed they just got worse. My ex didn't want to get divorced, but he had no intention of changing the way he was living his life. As I was advised, he was content. So the fact that I was unhappy was my problem. In his opinion, there were no happily married people, it was a façade.

After over a year of trying to mediate an agreement with this person who had become almost like one of the devil's minions in my eyes, I finally hired an attorney, had him served and got this show from off-Broadway to the main stage. I was tired of being strung along and played for the fool. My attorney was all about business and she also hated my ex. It was wonderful! She made me realize that I was at war and that resources I needed for the rest of my life were at stake. Mess this up, and you'll regret it for a long time. So I hired her and it was one of the best decisions I have *ever* made in my life.

I was building my team to help me win this fight. I had no idea how funky things would get. He countersued me. He tried to come off like the charming, debonair guy who was stuck with this woman who was trying to stifle his talent and creativity that rightfully belonged to the world. Well, my opinion was, set yourself free and get out of my life. But no, he wanted to drag this thing out!

Introduction

One day at work, as I sat in my cubicle he called to berate me about something. After the conversation I went in the bathroom to cry in a stall so no one could see me. Why was this happening to me, and why wouldn't he just get a grip and leave me alone? He didn't want me, shoot no man wanted me the way I was. Unhappy, depressed and totally twisted inside; I just wanted to get this thing over and try to figure out how I was ever going to be happy again.

Then someone walked in the bathroom. I tried to suddenly stop boo-hooing and get myself together. It was one of my kind-of work friends. She looked under the stall and saw my shoes and knew it was me.

"Wilma," she said. "Are you alright?" I opened the door and she saw my face with the tears streaming down it. She stepped into the stall with me and just hugged me.

She let me confide in her and then she told me something that shocked me. She had been where I was. She had been unhappily married and got divorced. But she was happy now. I thought to myself, what do I have to do to get there? How do I start living happier after?

A sort of, six-degrees-of separation process began at that point. My work friend from the bathroom told me of another person we knew who was divorced and living happier after. That person told me of another. Everyone's situation was a little different, some were remarried; others were happily single. Some lived with their mates in committed relationships. Others had a couple of guys they saw in different cities. Some weren't involved in relationships at all. But they all had a thought, recollection or story to uplift, inspire or prepare me. Those stories led me to start this book project with a blog and this first post at LivingHappierAfter.com/blog:

Today I'm on the road to living happier after. It's taken some time to get here; and one of many turning points was a chance encounter on a rainy DC evening when all I could think about was my long list of things to do. First on the list was a quick stop at the grocery store to get a few things for dinner.

Although it was the end of the day for my full-time office job, my briefcase was full of more work; and I was facing my second shift – that full-time job of nurturing my family.

While placing the items on the check-out stand my cell phone rings and I see from the name on the screen, it's my husband. We have a not so pleasant conversation. I end the call and somehow the cashier makes eye contact with me and says, "I remember those days of somebody always letting me down. That's why I divorced the bum".

I stood speechless for a moment. I knew that things weren't all good in my marriage, but did that conversation somehow trigger something for this lady?

And as she spoke to me, I started to really LOOK at her. I noticed the deep frown lines in her brow.

I saw that she was overdue to see her hairstylist, as the grey roots were obviously visible.

As she packed my food into the bags, I noticed her dry and wrinkled hands.

This lady did not look happy.

I asked her, "How long have you been divorced?"

"TEN YEARS", she said.

On the long ride home through the rain and terrible traffic I thought over and over about that grocery store cashier. I promised myself that day, not to end my life a bitter, unhappy woman, married or not!

Statistics document the fact that women initiate 65 percent of the divorces in America. In fact, among college-educated couples, 90 percent of divorces are initiated by wives! As women age they're deciding to leave unhappy marriages at rates never before seen in America. As Oprah said, "Fifty

Introduction

is the new thirty" and many unhappily married women are saying to themselves, "I have a lot of years of living to do, and I think I can be happier than I am now". As a result, the divorce rate among people over 50 has tripled in the past 20 years.

Fast forward a few years and I was there, over 40 and facing divorce. I began looking for books that would help me navigate the road from unhappily married to living happier after. I was looking for a book that focused on women who, alongside their husbands were "bringing home the bacon and cooking it, too" when their lives fell apart. I read lots of books, but could not find one that spoke to women in this space. I decided, now that I am 15 months post-divorce and getting happier every day, to write that book myself!

Many books served as an inspiration for me as I thought of writing a book about 'Living Happier After'. One in particular was a huge bestseller and was even made into a movie. Yes, I am referring to "Eat, Pray, Love" authored by Elizabeth Gilbert. Ms. Gilbert's book focuses on the year following her divorce as she travels to Italy, India and Indonesia and eventually finds love.

About six months into my separation I began to start my day by walking outside around the neighborhood for thirty minutes. It allows time for me to clear to my head and really manage my day. Like a lot of women I tend to 'over-think' situations and walking helps me to find my Zen. It also serves some other purposes, but those are for future blog posts :-)...Anyway, it seemed that the book about Ms. Gilbert's experiences was in my thoughts every morning. I wondered, what do women like me, who don't have the money, job skills or lifestyle to travel for a year to re-invent our lives after divorce do? And what about women like me *who have children and have to see and interact with our ex-spouse? How do we start living happier after?!*

I'm determined to be happier, no matter what. I know that there are other women who divorced and are living happier after. So I started talking to women (and men) about divorce and the strategies they or women they knew used to start living happier after. Many people told me about women who need to START living happily after and leave the past behind. So many people have encouraged me to take this project through to fruition. So here I go!

And here I am published author of the self-help book I was looking for during that period immediately following my separation and divorce.

Living Happier After is different than most divorce books. These are the thoughts of everyday women, not writers or actors, lawyers or financial wizards. They're folks like me and you. They did a lot of things right during that time, but they did some things wrong, too. They will tell you the ups and downs just like your real girlfriends would, if they'd been through it and used positivity to get out.

You don't want to be bitter. You want to get past it. You want to get to the good things in life for you. Then, listen to the conversation as women who, "refused to be stuck in that funky space" talk about how they got happier after their divorces. This book isn't trying to preach to you. The women aren't trying to teach you. They're trying to share their thoughts and uplift your spirits. No platitudes or grand pronouncements. I use pseudonyms, but trust that these are real women sharing real experiences and thoughts from that time to help you start living happier after, too.

Visit the website and join the community at www.LivingHappierAfter.com.

Chapter One

THE STRATEGIES

How do women get through the ugliness and desolation they feel in the immediate aftermath when their marriage ends? How do they move on from the incessant crying, anger, hurt and fear to living happier after their divorce? What tools do they use to change their lives and how long did it take?

I needed to know the answers to those questions. I wanted that information because I was at that exact point. My marriage had ended and I wanted to know how I *not* become the 'bitter bitch?' I felt I had every right to be one, but I knew that the path to future happiness did not include a stop at that station.

I don't have a lot of family that are divorced and the friends I knew who had faced this situation, I didn't feel comfortable asking those types of personal questions. Through a chance encounter, I discovered that some of the women I had made acquaintance with professionally over the years had been divorced, too.

Through conversations and interaction it became clear which of those women were really living happier after their divorces. Some pretended to be better, but when things got tough that inner 'b' came out strong. I mean everybody gets upset sometimes.

In contrast, however, the women living happier after took the blow; then they figured out how to make the situation work to their advantage, to their happiness. They handled the issues, but it was obvious they didn't see disaster around every corner, nor did they play the blame game, or 'woe is me' about every unpleasant or difficult challenge they faced in life. Somehow, it seemed they faced fewer of these problems than the other women did. Was one action dependent on the other for reaction? Dang, my curious mind wanted to know.

So I started reading as much as I could find about happiness. First the books:

The Happiness Project by Gretchen Rubin;

What Happy Women Know: How New Findings in Positive Psychology Can Change Women's Lives for the Better by Dan Baker Ph.D., Cathy Greenberg Ph.D. and Ina Yalof;

Eat, Pray, Love: One Woman's Search for Everything Across Italy, India and Indonesia by Elizabeth Gilbert;

The Pursuit of Happiness: Discovering the Pathway to Fulfillment, Well-Being, and Enduring Personal Joy by David G. Myers;

The How of Happiness: A New Approach to Getting the Life You Want by Sonja Lyubomirsky;

Happier: Learn the Secrets to Daily Joy and Lasting Fulfillment by Tal Ben-Shahar;

Choices That Change Lives: 15 Ways to Find More Purpose, Meaning, and Joy by Hal Urban;

A Short Guide to a Happy Life by Anna Quindlen;

Choosing Happiness: Keys to a Joyful Life by Alexandra Stoddard;

O's Big Book of Happiness: The Best of O, The Oprah Magazine: Wisdom, Wit, Advice, Interviews, and Inspiration by The Oprah Magazine Editors of O;

Choices: Taking Control of Your Life and Making It Matter by Melody Beattie;

The Strategies

Anyway: The Paradoxical Commandments: Finding Personal Meaning in a Crazy World by Kent M. Keith and Spencer Johnson;

Happiness: A History by Darrin M. McMahon; and

Happiness: Lessons from a New Science by Richard Layard.

I set up a Google Alert for the word happiness and also searched various versions of the term online. As a result, I read hundreds of blogs and articles, including 'The New Science of Happiness' by Claudia Wallis that was published by Time Magazine in 2004. It was there that I learned that Martin Seligman (who is currently Director of the Positive Psychology Center at the University of Pennsylvania) as the incoming president of the American Psychological Association in 1998, led the effort to spur the study of what became known as 'Positive Psychology.' The efforts of Dr. Seligman and other pioneers resulted in "an explosion of research on happiness, optimism, positive emotions and healthy character traits."

I then went to check out one of his books, 'Authentic Happiness: Using the New Positive Psychology to Realize Your Potential for Lasting Fulfillment.' In the book, Dr. Seligman breaks happiness down to three components: pleasure, engagement and meaning, with the latter two being 'much more important.'

Positive Psychology according to the Psychology Today website "examines how ordinary people can become happier and more fulfilled." So all this information overload made me wonder if the women who were living happier after divorce actually used these principles? So yes, the big mouth in me started talking with just a couple of the women I most trusted that I thought were living happier after divorce. I asked them, "Did you forgive your ex? How long after the breakup? How important was gratitude and doing things for other people when you first broke up?" One of the women told me about her feelings at that time and perfectly illustrated to me that I wasn't alone. It got the point across to me so succinctly. It made everything crystal clear regarding the choices she made.

This book was originally supposed to be about *my* journey to start living happier after divorce. After listening to that woman's experience I began to understand the advice I had been given months earlier that, 'including other women's stories' would make the book much more interesting. But would enough other women be willing to talk about that really ugly space in their lives from years ago?

On December 30, 2011, the Divorced Women's Happiness Survey (see Chapter 9) was launched online at SurveyGizmo.com. Using virtual word-of-mouth email from one divorced woman to another, over 100 women completed the survey. Thirty-four of those women self reported living happier after their divorces and documented using the principles of positive psychology to achieve their results. I was psyched! I was even more thrilled to discover than many of those women had provided their email contact information and agreed to be interviewed via telephone for the book.

I developed a script for the interviews to gather the women's thoughts, recollections and stories from that time in areas documented by positive psychologists as positively impacting one's happiness. As I read through my notes and clippings one quote from Marcus Buckingham, the author of 'Find Your Strongest Life' noted in a blog post on Huffington Post that, "Women who are happy simply decided they were going to be." He stated quite plainly what all those books I read used thousands of pages to explain. I knew I had to start there.

The longest chapter of stories in this book and the first question I asked the women was how did you manage your thoughts during that period when they realized their marriage was ending? The experts said the happiest women respond well when trouble strikes, have the confidence to know they can make it through, understand that most things they fear never come to fruition, take responsibility for their happiness, don't take everything personally, think positively, rid their mind of negative self talk and know that tomorrow will be better. Every one of these concepts is communicated by the women as they reveal their individual situations; the challenges they faced and how they overcame them. Or in some cases they tell you how they fell off the 'living happier after wagon,' and what they did to get back on.

The second question asked was if they did good things for other people without any expectation of something in return. Many of the psychologists documented that doing things for others made people feel their lives had meaning. A lot of the women, though not all, helped others and found it greatly impacted their happiness. They helped people they knew, some helped organizations and some helped animals. They found what fit for them and it made them feel better.

Next the women talked of nurturing relationships with God, family members and friends including forgiveness of their ex-husband and themselves.

Then the women spoke of engaging in activities that delight their senses like exercise, music, food, art, theater and more. They discuss the importance of doing things that make you lose yourself in them.

The next subject was one of the most important, according to the psychologists - gratitude. According to Dr. Seligman, gratitude was found as the "single most effective way to turbo charge your joy." In this chapter the women tell what they are grateful for and why. They also talk about forcing themselves to be happy with what they had at that time because they knew the universe had (and still has!) so much more for them.

Interestingly, my survey results did not find practicing gratitude to be the activity contributing the most to the divorced women's happiness. Gratitude was important, but their outlook on life was the biggest contributor to living happier after their relationship breakup.

To these women, the concept of living in the moment was addressed by exploring therapy, reflection and focus. They emphasized the fact that today is all you can be sure of and so they advise to be sure to attend to the process of doing small things everyday to lead to your overall goals.

Finally, they shared their ideas about the importance of saving time for themselves. How they go about saving a little bit of themselves, just for them, and the importance it has made to living happier after.

I interviewed women who graciously shared their stories, thoughts and recollections with me. Some shared more than others. Some women have contributions in each chapter, while others may only have shared in one area. Many of them provided background to assist in understanding their individual situations and why they made the choices they did.

One thing I need to advise is this is not a book bashing marriage or men. Every woman in this book, without exception or prompting stated they really wanted their marriage(s) to work. They gave it everything they had, but issues including abuse, desertion, financial disaster, infidelity, and some as simple, but important to a relationship as communication, eventually made divorce a way for them to start living happier.

This book is about giving women facing this situation one thing: *hope*. The expectation is that you'll find a connection. Somebody may have thought the same thoughts you are thinking now. When someone else was going through this time in their life, they may have faced the same issues you are dealing with. It's hard to find divorced women who have grown wiser and happier by the day willing to share their remembrances of tough times. Let this book be like finding that special group of super-positive girlfriends that always have your back. They have sister-wit and wisdom to share. I hope you enjoy and more importantly, I hope this book helps you get through the experience. We did it and I know *you* can, too!

Chapter Two

MANAGING YOUR THOUGHTS

Welcome to the gathering. Grab a comfortable seat and your beverage of choice; a cup of coffee, chai tea, a soft drink or perhaps a nice glass of wine. Let me introduce a group of wise and happy women. Listen to the conversation as each woman talks about learning to manage their thoughts when life as they knew it fell apart. Just like your real girlfriends, some tell you a lot, some just enough to let you know how they did it.

Problems range from simple things like communication to more serious matters involving abuse and deception. They were cheated on, beat on or told they no longer made him happy. Or he didn't care about her happiness.

Some men couldn't handle the stress or her success. Or she finally decided to remove those blinders and see her life for what it really was: fake and phony.

A few discovered they were repeating a pattern they learned long ago. Or they finally acknowledged the issue they knew had been there all along. High school sweetheart or dropout, PhD's to military officers and wives, the women pursue varied paths in life but share this important fact: managing your thoughts is the key to starting to live happier after divorce. No other factor matters as much.

Something So Simple

ADRIENNE

I met my husband when I was 21 and we dated for five years before we got married. Ten years into our marriage we had our son. We were together over twenty years. Everything in our life was planned and welcomed.

We had a good marriage, but at the core of our relationship, there was something wrong. You know how, even when you're young that something is not quite right? Something's not part of the puzzle and it's not all fitting together, but everything else is good, so you just ignore it.

When you're young and in the first years of marriage, you're busy and you're having fun. Then you go to child raising and rearing and you're super busy. All of a sudden my son was eight, and even though I was still busy, it's a different kind of busy than raising a toddler.

An inner voice kept saying to me, this relationship is not what you expected. I couldn't confirm if he was hanging out, but my suspicions told me that he was. When I asked, of course he said no, but something was not right. He was still doing his normal activities at home. He was taking care of his family and we were doing things together. We traveled, things were kind of like they always were, but I was unhappy.

My husband was a very introverted person and during the last ten years that started to drive me crazy. The older I became the more I felt I needed a partner I could talk to and have really good conversations with. He would never be that partner because he was always quiet and introverted. He was a good person. He took really good care of me and great care of our son. The internal part of the relationship, however, was never good for me.

He liked going out and doing things, but he didn't like having in depth conversations with people. When we would go to PTA meetings he would dread if someone were to ask him a question. He did not like social interaction that involved one-on-one conversations. We had lots of conversations, but there was never anything deep.

For instance, take 9/11. I work in the federal government contracting industry and when 9/11 happened, I came home ready to talk about it for days. He barely said a word. That started me thinking, this is not the person for me. We can't even talk about 9/11! What is it? He was only interested in pieces, here and there. The big scheme of what happened and why it happened didn't interest him. We never really talked about it. With specific events, that's the way things were all the time. On the other side, he got up in the morning and fed our son. He took him to school. He did all those things that make you love a husband and make him a good father.

The communication part just never quite worked. I think he sensed it. He should have because I talked about It all the time. I'd tell him, you don't talk enough. I need more communication. He became disenchanted with the fact that I complained about him all the time and I think he started hanging out.

When I tried to confirm what he was doing I could never quite figure it out. I could never catch him in the act. One day I was just fed up with him and the silent treatment. I was fed up with him in general. I remember I took a shower and I said, "God if this relationship is not meant to be anymore, please give me a sign." I blow dried my hair and went downstairs to get a glass of water. All of a sudden, his cell phone rang. I answered it and it was a woman who stammered, "S – S-Sorry, I have the wrong number." She didn't have the sense to just hang up. It was an indication to me that something was going on. I did a little research and started tracing phone numbers. I saw this number a lot.

Of course, when I confronted him he said nothing was going on. I told him whether it's going on or not we have a fundamental problem with communication. One thing led to another and I just kept shouting at him. I finally said, "We need to separate!"

It wasn't that easy. He was volatile and upset. Our son was upset. I came off as the selfish person. I made up my mind that I was at the age where I didn't have a lot of really good years left. I was over forty and I figured, if I'm going to find a partner who's going to make me happy, someone that I can communicate with, now is the time. I made up my mind to do just that.

Once we separated, I was miserable. I didn't even know how to function. I wondered what in the world I had done.

I was depressed about things like cutting the grass. I had two choices: either he could come over and cut the grass and badger me about all the things that we were arguing and fighting about at the time, or I could figure out how to cut that grass.

I was independent so things like working were never an issue for me because I had always made my own money. But I was depressed about little things like cutting the grass or taking the trash out. One day I looked out the window and saw that grass growing higher and thought should I call him? Or should I hire someone to cut it? Well, yeah I could, but I need the grass cut today. I was so depressed about that grass!

Managing Your Thoughts

I decided to get out the instruction book for our riding lawnmower. It took me two hours to figure out how to operate it. I backed that lawnmower out of the garage, and I cut the grass for the first time, *in my life*. I had never cut grass before. Can you believe that? We lived in that house for ten years. I did all kinds of other stuff, but I had never cut the grass.

After I cut that grass, I was like a new person. I felt independent. I no longer felt depressed. I took the trash out and pulled weeds. I did all the things that I thought I could not do.

Something so simple was life altering for me. It was life altering for him, too. Because when he came by and saw that I had cut that grass it was like the death of us. He knew it and as a result he wanted to move back in. He wanted to address our problem. I had asked him to go to a therapist to talk about the communication thing before we separated. He refused to do it, but after I cut the grass, he wanted to go to a couple's therapist. At that point it was too late.

I felt so much more independent. I knew what I wanted and I knew how to get it. I cut that grass every two weeks like a champ. Once when I began cutting it, my neighbors came out and said, "You go, girl!" Another neighbor watched. I was riding the lawnmower waving at people; I felt like Norma Rae. I was trimming and everything. It looked better than ever.

Looking For an Upgrade

VICKI

I believe that I was divorced in my heart and in my mind, no let me take that back, I was divorced in my mind long before the paperwork was signed.

I remember celebrating our fifth wedding anniversary and being so happy that we had passed the five year mark. Not that we didn't have problems, but we made five years. It wasn't perfect and I knew there was something there even before we went down the aisle, so I own a lot of it.

Our anniversary was in April. By August things were already starting to unravel, mentally and emotionally. He had expressed feelings of being threatened by my career and my relationships. This was during a period when I was beginning to take really good care of myself. 'Cause you know after you get married, you get lazy. You're happy and you start eating and you put on weight. I had started an exercise program and was watching what I ate. There were some occasions when I got attention from other men. I'm not sure it was jealousy on his part. It was more like 'this is another thing for me to be threatened by.'

He started to develop interests outside of the home. He was spending more and more time away from the house doing things he wanted to do with people that he wanted to do them with. It got to the point where there was no communication.

By the next year we were not even speaking to each other in the house. We were just two people having our own singular existence in the same dwelling. I spent months trying and trying to communicate. Trying to understand what the issues were because I didn't understand, or even believe that the issues were mine. I thought they were his.

I gave him a choice. His job required that he leave for 6-8 weeks to go to a different military base for maintenance of the plane that he was attached to. When he left I told him he needed to be different when he came back or be ready to separate.

When he came back nothing was different. No communication and no response to my ultimatum. Nothing. A few days later, I came home from work and there was a van parked outside the house and his friends were there moving stuff out. I walked up and asked, 'what was going on?' He had told them that things hadn't been going well and that we had mutually agreed to him moving out. They are looking at me and I was looking at them. I went upstairs to the bedroom and put my purse down. When I came downstairs, I started helping them move things out. I went into the kitchen and started taking half of everything that was in the cabinets, wrapping it up and putting it in boxes. If I'd have had a chainsaw like Madea in 'Diary of a Mad Black Woman,' I would have cut the couch in half!

His friends were looking at me, but I was not the least bit affected. I don't know what it was, but I helped them pack and get him out of the house. From that point on it really didn't matter. I was able to do that because I was mentally numb.

Over the next year or two I was trying to get the divorce process initiated and completed and there was no communication between us. I wondered if he didn't want to be with me, why wasn't he filing for divorce? I finally decided, if he's not going to file, then I'm going to file.

I wasn't going to be one of those people that have been separated for 50 years. If I find somebody that I am interested in, I don't want this to be a hindrance. You hear about people all the time that can't move forward, they can't get married and they can't make plans because one of them isn't divorced. I didn't want that. It was about having my freedom papers. I wanted to be removed from any legal liabilities because I didn't know what his crazy butt was going to do out there. I was already in enough financial stress. I wanted my name back and to be separated from him completely. That's what the paperwork was going to do.

So I filed and had him served. Then he wouldn't sign the paperwork. I was like alright, what else do I have to do? Months later one day, magically the paperwork appeared in the mailbox, signed and it was done.

I want you to know that there was almost no communication during that time. We only had one conversation between the day he left the house and today. That's when I tracked him down to ask why he hadn't filed. I guess emotionally or mentally he was out of it, too. Maybe he had been out of it longer than me.

If I had to start the process and go through the grieving process, emotionally, mentally and all of that stuff at the same time, I am sure it would have been more difficult. I count it as a blessing that my head was out of it a long time before my heart. It didn't take my heart long to catch up.

To manage my mind during that time, I began to consider myself single because it was just about the piece of paper at that point. I was doing my best to do what I was supposed to do, but in my mind, I was single. That's how I managed through.

I placed a lot of attention on me because I always knew that I was meant to be married. I knew I wasn't meant to be out in the world alone. A lot of people get divorced and say, 'I'm never doing that again!' I never thought that. I knew I hadn't been with the right person, but I had to find or either lay in wait for the right person to be sent to me.

I spent time focusing on me to make sure that I was ready if and when God presented that person. I didn't want the marriage baggage; what he did and how he acted and all of that. I was looking for an upgrade in a man; I needed to be able to present myself as an upgrade. That meant a healthy lifestyle; in what I eat, how I manage my activities, including working out and just having a positive attitude about things. A big part of that was a celibate lifestyle. I had already kissed enough frogs. The next one needs to be a prince. I'm not kissing anymore frogs!

From a spiritual standpoint it was like, 'Oh so you want to receive the right person? Well, you need to be ready for the right person. Don't waste yourself.' And it was OK, because you find other things to fill that void.

It Wasn't Even About Me

CYNTHIA

My story may not be unique, but it felt that way to me. I was married for about two years and my then-husband was planning a big career move. We were going to be relocating. So I traveled to the city where we were planning to move to, to look at houses and day care for our child, who was a toddler at the time. The plan was all coming together. We discussed the move and made long-term plans. One night shortly before the move, we made love in front of the fireplace. The next morning was typical as I got up and went to work, as usual. When I came home from work, however, he was gone!

Clothes gone. Possessions gone.

He left a note on the stove saying that he just couldn't do it anymore. So how was I managing my thoughts? After that, I think I cried for a full forty-eight hours. When my 1 ½-year-old son wasn't with me, I just boo-hoo'd and when he was with me, mommy was fine. As soon as he went to sleep, my composure was gone.

For two days I could hardly function. I was in a fog. He had disappeared! I didn't know how to reach him for three full weeks! All I had was a letter. I'm wondering, 'did he kill himself?' The letter was vague, "I can't do this anymore." His family didn't know where he was. His friends didn't know where he was.

When he resurfaced about three weeks later, he had an apartment. He had moved into a place in the city where we used to live together. Within two weeks after resurfacing, his then girlfriend who became his second wife, moved in with him. Talk about managing my thoughts! I went from anger to sadness to anger to fear, but anger was a common feeling.

I felt I was the last to know. Clearly this was a plan and had been in play for quite some time, but nobody bothered to tell me. Remember we had these long term plans for our life and I thought we were acting on them.

When I got past the initial anger, I realized that it was done. It didn't take long though, because he was clear that it was done. All of my thoughts were focused on, what did I do? What happened? What clues did I miss? I didn't really feel I had done anything wrong, but somewhere along the way, I wasn't really aware of what was happening in my own life. It was hard to move on because I was still trying to figure out what the hell happened.

I begged and pleaded with him to go to a counselor with me. He said he would go, but only so he could help me move on. During the counseling session he said, "I'm just not happy, and I have a right to be happy and so I am going to be happy."

The counselor asked, "What did your wife do to make you unhappy?"

He said, "Nothing, I'm just not happy." I don't think he had an answer.

Once I realized this wasn't even about me, I decided to pick myself up and dust myself off. It clearly wasn't what I thought it was, and if it wasn't what I thought it was, I had nothing to miss.

About three years after he left us, he and his wife moved out of the country. I didn't see him for almost two years. That helped quite a bit. He was so far away that we didn't have to communicate a lot.

When he returned to the states, he emailed and we set up dates and drop locations so he could see our son.

When our son was older, he would read his letters from his dad and peck out a reply. Because it was so expensive we would only call once in a while. The distance helped me manage my thinking because you have to move on. You have to figure out a way to be whole within yourself because this little person is looking at you. You are *it* for him because now his father is gone. You are just going to have to pull it all together.

Fast forward to now. We've been separated and since divorced for almost 19 years and now have a great relationship. It's only because I got to a point where I recognized, I may never know what happened. He has never explained to me what happened and he's never apologized for it. I worked through all my feelings about it because we had a child together.

He and his second wife, who he ended up divorcing, had a child together. She and I had a very rough relationship when they returned to the states. I tried to put up a barrier and she tried to be friendly, and I thought overly affectionate with my son. I thought she was trying to take my place. That messed me up for a while. Then I realized, 'why are you upset that someone loves this little person who is actually a nice kid?' Of course, she loves him. He's a great little guy.

Managing my thoughts was all about what do I need to do to move on from where I was. I just refused to be stuck in whatever that funky space was.

I Love You

CAMILLE

My husband was a cheater and couldn't keep it in his pants. The lady that he cheated on me with looked like a cross between Celie from 'The Color Purple' and Wesley Snipes' character in 'To Woo Fong' in drag. I was a hard worker and a good wife. I took care of the kids. I went to work and I was taking college courses in the evening. I thought I was doing everything right. In the end, I felt like he wanted a submissive woman, a woman that didn't have a mind of her own. When I found out he was cheating and that my brother was involved, I was devastated and hurt.

I remember lying in bed having that talk with God about whether to kick them both out of my house. I couldn't believe my brother would help my husband cheat by covering for him and lying to me. I thought about my husband, 'what am I getting out of this relationship?' I pay my own bills. I cut my own grass. I take care of my kids. It's as if I'm doing it all myself. I got up and packed their bags and put both of them out of my house at the same time.

I started to read self-help books. One of the things I learned was you have to love yourself. One technique to reinforce this is to stare at yourself in mirror in the morning and don't just stare at your reflection, but look yourself in the eye and tell yourself, "I love you." It goes a long way. If you learn to love yourself then you don't need to worry about how he betrayed your love. Or how do I move on to the next relationship?

    I started to focus on me. I had gastric bypass surgery and lost 125 pounds. I made a promise to myself to always take care of myself and not to forget about me again. In my marriage, I lost myself. I was so focused on being a good wife, mother, hard worker and a good provider, that I was kicked to the background. Hair, nails, none of that mattered.

    I don't focus on having a man or needing someone beside me anymore. I go to the movies by myself. I take my Kindle and go to happy hour by myself. My self-worth is more important than anything a man can offer. I've learned to speak up and to love myself for exactly who I am. If I work hard on improving and taking care of myself then I don't have to worry about anything else. It'll come. God has it all worked out for me.

Dad Never Says Nasty Things

MELISSA

One evening my 15-year-old son pointed out how poorly I was handling life after separation, even though I'm the one who said that I was unhappy and had to get out. My ex wasn't spending time with our kids the way that he should have been. On this day he spent three or four hours with the boys, took them to dinner and then brought them back instead of keeping them overnight. I really needed the extended time to get myself together. The lack of 'me' time was one of the reasons I was having such a hard time managing my thoughts.

I said something unkind about his father and he replied, "You know, when we're with dad he never says nasty things like that about you."

I thought to myself, I guess he doesn't have to. I mean he is with you two for dinner once a week for 3 hours. I'm with you every other moment except when you're in school. He's living the single life, out with his women and I am here raising you. I didn't express my thoughts out loud, thank the Lord. But I was so twisted inside. Whether I stayed with him or not, I felt like he was still screwing me.

I hadn't thought about the emotional part of the separation process. I considered the financial, social, legal and other aspects, but not how my emotions would swing from one extreme to the other, flinging me along with them! In that moment, I decided to get back to a healthier place emotionally.

I ended my marriage after trying to do everything I could to save it. But one person can't save a marriage. I read a self help book that tells you to be ruthlessly honest with yourself about whether the people in your life are about positivity and making your lives better. I knew my life wasn't like that.

Months after I read that book, I read it again and read it again. I finally built up the nerve to end my marriage. There were a lot of other things that gave me the support I needed, like my employer's Employee Assistance Plan. I was eligible for unlimited telephone therapy 24/7 with a counselor and I called many times and spoke with trained professionals who talked me off the proverbial ledge. That was such a blessing because they gave me techniques that helped me see my relationship was headed into a ditch at a high rate of speed. Finally, I did it.

Then six weeks into the separation and my son was telling me that I wasn't doing a real good job of this. So I made a concerted effort not to be so critical. I knew that I had to get through it and that there was no going back. That's what my ex was waiting for, for me to come back. He thought that in spite of me being a strong person, my high paying job and many accomplishments, I wouldn't be able to move forward without him.

When we were together, I stopped managing my thoughts appropriately. My attention was focused on him, and then my children. My needs were not a priority. It was hard for me to even consider doing for myself until I realized that I had lost him. He was focused on someone else.

Managing Your Thoughts

One night when he was out until 4 or 5 in the morning I had a nightmare. It was the most realistic nightmare I've ever had. My husband was making love to another woman and I was standing in the room watching. It was so real to me and it shook me to my core. I think it was probably true and it was something that God sent me to try to show me that I needed to move on.

Each of these things helped moved me toward a decision to manage my thoughts for me and to get myself back. I focused on me and my sons and stopped letting someone else control me, just because I loved them. I cut back on negative radio and TV and I stopped being around negative people. I started walking 10,000 steps every day, meditating and being thankful.

As I focused more on positive things, more positive experiences came into the lives of me and my children. I stopped focusing on what their dad wasn't doing. I decided that I *am* the better woman and I needed to start proving it.

One of my colleagues told me about her parent's divorce. She spoke admiringly of her mom's behavior during the time that they were co-parenting her siblings and herself. She said, "My mom was my, 'She-ro'." I decided that's what I wanted to be for my sons. I also reached out to my ex-husband's children from his first marriage. They are grown, but they have been a part of my life for almost 20 years and I love them, too.

I believe I started on the road to living happier by the force of my own thoughts. Nothing more.

All about Me

TERESA

For eighteen months, I was dumbfounded, sad and unable to function. I couldn't get over what had happened to me and I cried at a moment's notice. I never envisioned that for me and I took it so personally. Obviously, I had some things I had to work on.

The man I married made me think the problem was me. Quite honestly, it was. When I found out that my spouse was cheating with not one, but three women only eighteen months after our wedding I was pissed. He had done everything to win my love. Now I was crushed because I had placed my value on being his wife. I had to find out for myself that I must be internally focused, not externally focused.

I had allowed someone else to determine my self-worth. That was a revelation for me. After that, my life became all about me. I worked out every day because I knew that I had to keep myself together and still do the things that made a difference to me. Every time I worked out I cried about something different. Finally, I was able to give up all of the anger and resentment.

I realized I have to have a sanctuary where I can be happy and fulfilled. Because I don't have any children, it's my home, my friends and my family. I have pulled it all together and I am safe here. I have built a place of pleasure for me. That's very important and it allowed me to finally get rid of the anger and the bitterness. I stopped asking why me. It all happened for a reason.

I felt like I was in the Marines. When you're in the Marines everyone gets beat down so they can be built back up. That's exactly what I went though. I felt like I had to go to my own ground zero and build myself back up. It was the most grueling and the most fabulous thing I've ever done. It was fabulous because it gave me a reason to look inside and find myself. I've been defined by other people my entire life and now I define me.

Run It Out

LISA

I can't say my divorce happened because it was one person's fault. We were both in it together. Sometimes you pick people and then realize things aren't working out. You try really hard to make it work because there was love there, but as we uncover our faults, you figure out how heavily it's impacting your relationship.

My ex-husband had a lot of insecurities from his youth. He didn't have a good relationship with his father. He internalized it all and didn't communicate well. He tried to self-medicate and I think he also suffered from depression. When he got upset and had to communicate, especially after we had the baby, he became very negative and sometimes verbally abusive. When it was over, he'd say he was sorry. It became a pattern. Intellectually, I understood that he was insecure, but I got to the point that I didn't want to take it.

The situation started to get worse. He would get a little physical. The abuse began chipping away at my feelings. I started feeling negative about myself. I knew we needed to get some help. I didn't realize how bad things had gotten until we started counseling. He admitted he had done some pretty bad things. After we had been going to counseling for a while he gave the counselor and I the finger during a session and walked out. That was the end.

I understood depression on some level because my mom suffered with it, but we never talked about it. Maybe that's why I married him. Anyway, I decided that I had to work on me and figure out why I picked this person. We started the separation agreement when our son was a year old. Six months later we were divorced.

The whole thing was very overwhelming. I used to run a lot so I decided to begin training for a marathon. Preparing for the marathon kept me from going crazy. I took the baby in the baby jogger and we went out all the time, even on really long runs.

I joined an AIDS Awareness group that ran. We ran all the time and trained up to 18 miles. We even ran across the finish-line together at the marathon. Running helped me get a baseline, stabilization, so I could get the angst out, you know?

I cried every day for two years. It was terrible. But I developed goals, I wasn't consumed by it. I had something physical that could get rid of all the stress.

I also attended cognitive therapy for four years. It taught me to think myself out of situations. I would ask myself what's the worst case scenario and then I would see, I'm still here, I'm still alive, and then I would just calm down because I understood it's not the end of the world. Then I would figure out what I was going to do.

You're supposed to think of your past, all the things you've been through. It gets easier as you get older and have experienced some things. You tell yourself all of the things you've been through to calm yourself down. Those techniques were really useful. I learned to understand my mom's depression and what was happening with my ex-husband. I learned to understand myself and that I am kind of a co-dependent. I joined an Al-Anon group, and went to Al-Anon meetings every week. That's how I learned to manage my thoughts.

When I get in a rut or I'm not taking care of myself, I think, 'You need to work out more.' I think my way through things. When I run

Living Happier After

I start off with all this stuff in my head. By the time I'm done, my thoughts are clear. The ones that mean nothing get pushed out and you're left with a couple of things to deal with and it seems more manageable.

Fit the Mold

TAMRA

As I was going through my separation and divorce I realized there was perpetual negative self-talk when I was around my ex and I was the victim. I was always the victim—of his behavior, of his choices and everything he did.

I've done a lot of psychological, mental and spiritual study and I recognized a pattern in my life. It started in my relationship with my father and I repeated it with every man prior to my husband. So the relationship with my husband wasn't new, he just fit the mold. Though he wasn't 'like' my father in every way, he had the same energy my father carried.

My father was an abusive man to my mother. He was the kind of man who had to own all the space, my mother was rendered powerless in his presence. My ex-husband was never physically abusive, but his energy was oppressive. If he was upset, he would withdraw from me. We couldn't talk about things and work things out. I was afraid to do things and afraid to make choices. I was constantly worried about what he would do or how he would feel about it. I was worried about whether he would punish me by taking his love away, taking his approval away, like I was a child in some way.

Once I realized that pattern throughout my life, I was able to begin to heal, starting with my father. It changed *everything*. I gained a different perspective of my father and started thinking differently about him. I began to understand why he was the kind of person he was. I realized that I wasn't a victim and I got to choose how I would respond. I am not powerless and my mother wasn't powerless either, even though she was abused. She chose to be in an abusive relationship. She chose to allow him to treat her the way that he did. She got something out of that; there was an exchange going on, there was an agreement between the two of them.

The same applied between me and my ex-husband. I was not a victim. I was playing out sort of a psychological, mental and emotional paradigm that I learned from my parents.

Once that changed, everything shifted. It took a while to get to that point and it was after we had divorced. He was the one who left and divorced me. It took time to get to the point where I was able to begin to speak my truth to my ex-husband in a way that didn't feel like I was fighting for my life. Then I was able to tell him what I thought about things, what worked for me, what didn't work and what my needs were. We still run into bumps and I become fearful and start to feel like a child again. But now I'm able to recognize what's going on; I am not a little girl and he is not my keeper. I get to say what I need, to speak my truth and we treat each other like adults.

This has served me in a great way. It really adds to my happiness because I am being myself in a way I never have with my ex-husband or any man. So, it's really, really good.

Break That Mold

SHEREE

Everything I did at that point was driven by the love of my kids. My eldest son said to me one day out of the clear blue sky, "Leaving dad was the best thing you could have ever done for us." I began to take on my share of the guilt wondering why I stayed for so many years. The kids and I walked on eggshells around their dad for a long time. It wasn't until we were no longer with him that we realized it.

I did a self examination of myself, sort of self therapy and I played videos in my head of my parent's marriage. My mother lost herself trying to please my dad. I made up my mind that I was going to break that mold. I was not going to be my mother all over again in a situation that was detrimental to me and my kids. I was determined to bring closure to my mother's world.

I began to speak positively and I began to dream. I began to visualize myself in places that I never thought I could be as a single mother or a single woman. I held on to my dreams and the promises of God. I changed my direction away from my mother's world and learned to learn to manage my thoughts. I was determined not to re-live my mother's mistakes.

Owe It to Essence

PEGGY

My ex-husband was eleven years older than me. He was more of a Svengali, more father figure than an equal mate or a peer. He taught me a lot, but he also stifled my growth.

One time I said, "So I think I want to go shopping and buy an outfit for the party we're going to this weekend."

He said, "Well, wait a minute, who told you to think?"

I was orphaned more or less and a ninth grade dropout because my mom died young and my dad was out there. My husband was all I had.

A friend who lived nearby introduced me to Essence magazine. Reading that magazine helped me grow up. I became a young woman and started having thoughts of my own because of what I read in Essence.

I started thinking my relationship didn't seem right. For many years it was all I knew, but I started realizing that it wasn't right because it didn't have me in it. I would tell him I was hungry. He'd say, "I ate at the same time as you and I'm not hungry so you can't be hungry." That's the way it was.

Managing Your Thoughts

It took nine months to plan my escape and sneak away. Ending the relationship was the first chance I had to think for myself. It took a lot for me to have thoughts of my own. I was afraid of him, physically, mentally and everything else. But I started thinking for myself and I really owe that to my girlfriend and Essence magazine. That's the truth.

Nothing to Compare

DANIELLE

After my marriage ended, I spent the majority of my time focusing my thoughts on me. Before that I was completely consumed with thinking about how to destroy my ex. Twenty-four hours a day I was thinking about how I could hurt him as much as he hurt me.

I think it's important to tell you a little about how I grew up. I am an only child and both of my parents were only children. I used to think nothing of it, but over the years I discovered that oneness is very significant. It affects your perspective and it affects how things are done.

I was raised primarily by my grandparents, and I never lived under the same roof as my mother. My mother was career oriented and my grandmother encouraged her to pursue her career and that's what she did. I never really had a close bond with my mother, even though she was around all the time. My grandmother was like my mother. I wouldn't call my family affectionate, there was no huggy-kissy and encouragement, it was business as usual.

I lived in a house where it was very uncomfortable for me to bring friends over. Families had to be screened. 'Who are they, where are they from? We don't know them. They can't come in here.' There was a lot of loneliness and very few outlets for me to express myself.

I had my first intimate relationship at 24 with the man who would become my husband. He was in the armed forces at the time and we hit it off immediately. I was looking for love in all the wrong places. I didn't even know what love was. I had nothing to compare it to, so I fell, hook, line and sinker. Several months into the relationship I got pregnant. I didn't want to go home because I wasn't married. But I went home anyway. My grandmother figured it out, she was one of those people with the crystal ball. My mother was livid. She always had an ideal of what I should be and who I should become. I never quite hit the mark as far as my mom was concerned.

I was 24 years old and a college graduate and the typical parent's response would be 'you're an adult so you are going to have to figure this out.' Not my mother, she wanted to take full control of the situation. I decided then, I was getting married. He had already asked me, so we did just that. After the first baby, 22 months later, came another, then 22 months later another, and then 22 months later, a fourth child was born.

As our children were being born our relationship was quickly changing. He was 15 years my senior. What I saw as an extremely romantic, earth shattering type of relationship quickly turned into something that was dark and unknown to me. I take the blame for a lot of that because I was so sheltered and naïve. I hadn't taken the time to discover how I was changing. Throughout my life I felt so much pressure to live up to other people's expectations. I was always trying to be what others thought I should be.

He was my prince charming. He was the man that was going to sweep me off my feet, take me away from all my disappointment, all my loneliness and wandering. My whole life, everything about me, everything that I had was wrapped up in that relationship. There was nothing else. I somehow felt fulfilled and didn't need anything else. I didn't need a career or all the other things that my girlfriends were going for at the time. It didn't matter to me. I thought that I had everything because I had four kids and a husband.

Then he got out of the service. One day it occurred to me that he hadn't gone to the base for a few days. I finally asked him why. He said he had been discharged. I asked him why he didn't discuss this with me, why wasn't this a joint decision? He said to me, "Under no circumstances are you ever to think that I'm going to discuss anything with you, or to include you in any decisions that I make regarding anything." I was stunned.

I had to think about that for a minute. There weren't enough names that I could call myself when I looked back and realized that I had never been involved in any major decision that happened in that relationship. He had never asked me anything. He was doing his thing and being who he was, but I didn't even know who that was. All I knew was that I had my four little kids and I was playing with them and watching Sesame Street. I thought that was the way marriage and home life were supposed to be. I didn't know the difference.

I looked at him and saw a stranger.

When he told me no, you're not included, you're not a part of what I do, and the decisions that I make, that snapped me to attention. It changed me and I became an instigator at that point. I wanted to know everything that happened for the last ten years. What's up with this? What's up with that? Why is this the way it is?

I began to understand who he was, an incredibly mean man. Everyone around me told me that about him before we got married, but I never saw it. I definitely had blinders on.

Life Is Too Short

Kathy

I began to manage my mind as I anticipated leaving him. I had to get in the right mindset because I had two kids and I wasn't really certain about the outcome. I have a one hour commute to my job and that became my hour of prayer. I asked God to help me.

It took me about three years to stop the crying and feeling like, I can't believe this crap has happened to me. The passing of my cousin made me realize life is too short to be living the way I was. My husband would drink on the weekends and beat me. It didn't happen in the beginning of our marriage, but it was a regular occurrence after about ten years. I hid it from almost everyone, I thought. But my kids knew. I didn't want them to think that their dad beating me was right. My cousin's death and my children were my onset to wake up and realize that I needed to roll.

I quietly bought things that I needed for my new home. When we left I took all my stuff with me and set the house up for him. I don't know why, I guess that's me, but that's how I managed myself. I knew I'd be fine after I left because I had my kids and they are my power.

Living Happier After

I know it's going to be better tomorrow because I have God, plain and simple. That is my strength. My happiness is my children, my work and my friends. My friends keep me in line and when I need to talk with them, I do. Sometimes I see that fork in the road and I wonder which way to go. I know that I'm going in the direction that I need to.

I am happier after marriage even though I don't have a relationship right now. I have learned that I only pick men who are not good for me. I decided I am better off alone for the time being. When I am with someone I am upset and stressed out so having the calmness of being at peace is more important, it's a wonderful thing. It is something I always sought and now I have it. My kids are grown, I live in my home alone with my dogs and life is good. I am extremely happy the way I am.

There Is Life After

KIM

I came to the realization that I was a single parent and I was scared. When my ex-husband and I separated, my emotions were all over the place. I had a home with him, a mortgage, car note, day care, and two young children. My sons were five and one year old at the time.

I prayed to God and asked him to help me. I needed strength to endure this because I no longer have my spouse. God did just that. He strengthened me even more.

Even though I was already a strong person I knew that I needed help. I am very thankful to my parents, God rest their souls, and my brother who were very influential in my children's lives. We've always been a close-knit family and I owe a lot to my father and my brother for being male role models for my sons. They taught them what I could not teach them.

Every year there was a challenge. When we first separated each time major problems would happen I would think, 'I can't do, I can't do this.' I continued to do my best through the tears, through the heartache and through the pain. I loved my kids and I wanted the best for them. During their childhood, adolescence and teenage years, there was very little support from their dad. There was so much I had to do on my own. It bothered me and because of the lack of support I didn't want to be around him too much.

I continued to hold on with strength from my family because I trusted that my life would get better in spite of what was lacking in the family. Now years later my sons have graduated from high school. My oldest son is 23 years old and he's been in the U.S. Marine Corps for four years. My other son graduated high school and is interested in the Marine Corps as well.

I am very thankful to God. During the time I took care of my sons, I focused on them and sacrificed for their well-being. I didn't go out too much because my most important goal was making sure that *they* were taken care of. I have no regrets when it comes to that. They were my priority and the end result is that they're taking care of me. We're still a close-knit family. There is life after. There is love after.

The Freedom of Lifting

ALEXIS

It felt as if I was carrying a weight around. I was trying to make another person see more of who he was and what he could become in the world. I realized I couldn't change someone in that way. It was a realization that the weight I put on him wasn't the life he wanted to live.

I gained a sense of freedom by lifting that obligation from my ex and was able to then manage my thoughts. I recognized that our worlds couldn't co-exist. Coming to that realization put me in a mental state where I could release him. I think being alone allows you to center on yourself and heal yourself. I recognized that it was me in the world, so I needed to take care of me.

What You Create

TAYLOR

I made managing my thoughts a priority. I had to train my thoughts to be focused on what I wanted, not what I didn't want. I had to get in the mode where I was ready to shift forward. If I stayed where I was I was just going to attract more of what I already had.

If it's how your attorney treats you in the process or the next mate you attract, if you don't shift the way you think, you may change partners or move out of that particular situation, but you'll remain stuck in that mental space. I had to make that an enormous priority and monitor my thoughts all the time. A good question I asked myself was, 'do I want more of this?' If the answer is no, then what do I want? Instead of focusing on whatever the icky thing is, I focus on what I would love in its place.

This is a really sensitive, delicate time when you're creating this new way of being in the world. Creating your new vision for a world that includes the things you actually do want is a really fragile place to be. It takes time to make the habit stick.

I looked at the people around me and the messages they were giving me. I wanted to stay in a positive place and to think about things in those terms. That was what I wanted to draw into my now.

Managing Your Thoughts

I began focusing on the good and the beautiful that are possible for me.

That can mean withdrawing from some of the people in your life.

My mom has always been a worrier and she taught me to worry. When she realized that I was not coming from that place, she felt like she had to double or triple her worrying efforts. 'Oh my goodness, you're not worried, how could you not be worrying about these things?'

I've found that when you worry it draws more of what you're worrying about to you. I told her very clearly, "Mom, I love you and I know that you have good intentions for me, but if you continue to focus on the negative, I am going to have to stop having these telephone conversations with you." I told her in advance, "If the negativity starts happening, I will tell you, mom, I'm hanging up now. I will just put the phone down and there will be no further discussion." I told her I would just say it and do it, and I did, a couple of times. After that, she would catch herself and I could hear it. She'd be about to say something and I would kind of start to giggle because I would know. She managed to stay with me on the journey although there were other friends who didn't. Some of them I have resumed a relationship with, and some I haven't.

In addition to monitoring your thoughts, there's also the kind of thought environment that you put yourself in. A lot of women like to tell the stories about the horrible thing that happened to so-and-so when she was going through her divorce. I didn't want to become a part of that because I didn't want that to be what I created for myself.

Worth a Lot

KANDI

It's been ten years on the other side for me. People at work ask me, why I'm so happy, and why I smile so much. If they only knew where I was ten years ago; I feel so blessed. Self-esteem was the biggest factor for me because my ex had mentally abused me. I didn't think I was worth anything. I didn't think anybody else could love me. He made a big deal out of any little thing I did wrong and he looked down on me. "I can't believe you did this." It didn't matter how small it was, it really tore me down. Later in life, I realized he did that because of his own issues.

Moving to another place helped me manage my thoughts. When I was a program manager I overheard a conversation and learned that my employer needed a sales rep in another region. The person that they want to take the job didn't want to go, so I said, "I'll take it." I was thinking I could relocate and be able to keep my salary. If I stayed in the area I would have to see him regularly and he would continue to try to tear me down. I knew I had stayed in the relationship too long. He kept saying to me, "How can you do this to the kids?" Toward the end I would drive up to our house after work and sit in the car in tears because I did not want to go inside. It was that bad.

By the end we walked around the same house and he would not utter a word to me. This was because I made a couple of decisions without him. I finally started seeing the things my mom and other people were telling me. Then I started acting out, as he would say. He was like, "OK, oh wait a minute, what done changed?"

But you know what really helped me through all this? I joined a small church. Being at that church gave me an outlet; that really helped.

Surround Myself with Positive

GRETCHEN

My situation had to take me down before I could begin to rebuild. I supported my ex for twelve years, then he went and screwed around, that's just one of those things I can't abide.

He stuck me with everything financial and I was angry. I was angry at myself primarily because I'm not a stupid woman. How did I allow that to happen? Of course, I was also mad at him, but the whole thing was pretty much directed at me.

I managed my thoughts in a lot of different ways and I tell you, it was not organized at all. It was more of a day-by-day thing and sometimes minute-by-minute. I got an apartment in a new city. When I moved all I had was my dog and my computer. I had to order a bed. The first night I slept on the floor. I'm the daughter of a doctor and always had money. I thought I would always have money. Getting separated and moving from a huge house with lots of money and things, to having $12,000 in my checking account and everything I own in an apartment; I was scared to death!

I did a lot of walking and as a result I lost a lot of weight. I surrounded myself with positive things and that's when girlfriends really came into play. I have this one special girlfriend, who was troubled that I used to always stay home. She picked me up and said, "Let's go. We're going out shopping to get all the things that you need for your new home."

I surrounded myself with really good friends and we didn't necessarily talk about my problems, but I knew I wasn't alone. Normally I don't really care, I'm usually pretty self-sufficient. During this time, however, I needed to know there was someone else there.

I was also in a leadership group so I didn't feel like such a failure. During the same time that we split up, my father died and I closed down my business. I had no husband, no job, and no father, who was actually the rug underneath my feet, but I didn't know that.

I had to go through the steps you experience during a loss. I had to go through every single one of them and some I had to go through several times. I read a lot of self-help books to try to understand what a professional woman who has all of a sudden found herself in this situation does.

I had to be judicious about my money. I met a whole bunch of new friends. One lady was a yoga teacher and she invited me to her class. I didn't have to pay too much, because she said, "Oh just come on in!" That helped a bit.

I did the dating scene some and I've got to tell you, those were, my "*ho*" years. In twenty years of marriage, I never screwed around and all of a sudden, I'm meeting guys. I'm saying, "Hey, that's interesting. They find me attractive!"

It really has to do with the positive thoughts, even though sometimes it was very difficult to have positive thoughts.

We Just Outgrew One Another

JACQUELINE

My ex was my high school sweetheart and I was a virgin when I met him. We had a long history together.

After my father died my ex allowed my mom to come into our house after she got sick. At first, I would go to her house to help her. She suffered from heart problems and diabetes and had a lot of medications. She was married to my dad for forty-something years and it was hard for her to move on. My ex built a mother-in-law suite at our house and I think it gave her extra years of life. I still appreciate and respect him for what he did.

After she died, we pretty much realized she was the glue keeping us together, but it didn't hit us until then. I think if we were adult enough, we would have seen we just outgrew one another, or our paths were no longer the same.

One thing is sort of unusual in my situation. The children usually go with the mother. I allowed my children to stay where they wanted to be and they did not want to leave their home. I think sometimes when you're going through a divorce, adults can be selfish. Because I am the mother this child is going to go with me. Have you thought about asking the child what they want? We did that and to my shock, well, not shock, but you know…their family was nearby and so that's where they stayed.

My ex and I just grew apart. We weren't on the same level as far as our life, we were just not synching as one in a partnership. We didn't like the same types of things except for maybe going to jazz festivals or things like that. He was almost a recluse. I was involved with my music and it kept me going. He was jealous of all of the things I was involved in. I tried to include him in those things, but I don't think that was enough.

As women, we tend to reach out further than men do when it comes to relationships because we want it to work. We do whatever we can to try to make it work because you want to have that loving home. I wasn't actually looking to get a divorce.

I joined the church and I wanted him to be a part it. His father would say things like, "you know the church is just another institutional business"' A lot of his father's thinking about the church influenced him, so he didn't want to go for that.

There was one other thing about the church; a lot of times when you're going through these things, my situation is not going to be your situation and your situation is not going to be my situation. There were too many people trying to give me some damn advice when they did not know my situation. Church folks, especially older church women telling me, "Don't you leave that house! I been with my husband 45 years, and I'm sleeping in one room and he's sleeping in another, and everything is just fine."

Well, that may be fine for you, but that's not the way that I wanted my life to be. I didn't care about material things. I wanted a life. I don't have to own a home. That ain't identifying who I am. Especially, if I am all-heartbroken. You think I'm gonna stay up here in that? That sounded like a cold, bitter life and I didn't want that.

Living Happier After

In order for me and anybody around me to be happy, I have to be happy with me.

Once the decision was made, I finally realized I had to live for myself. I had to stop pretending and acting like everything was wonderful and great when it really wasn't. My life was ok, my job was fine; from the outside looking in everything was OK. But there was a division there. Before I moved, we sheltered the kids a lot; we didn't want them to know.

When I moved into my apartment the kids thought it was fun. They had a new place to go and we'd have a good ole' time when they would come over on the weekends. Even though we were apart they knew Mama was there. They could pick up the phone and call me for anything. That's what kept me going. That first year without my babies though, oh my God, I had some moments. I cried because I didn't have my children with me. They were eight and twelve years old at the time and that was very hard for me. When we did see each other, we really had quality time. When you're with them 24/7 sometimes they go their way, you would go yours. Now, however, we knew we only had the weekend and then they'd have to go. We made it quality and cherished that time together.

The success of the whole arrangement is reflected in my daughter and son today. Of course, there's going to be a little damage because of the divorce, but there's a little damage when all of you are together. Especially if it's ugly, and there's no love going on up in the house and children start seeing that craziness.

I think about it sometimes and if I had it to do over again I would do the same thing. I have no regrets with the way things turned out.

A Real Spoiled Brat

CAROLINE

I'll try to remember as best I can because this was a while ago. One of the first things other than my own initial shock, disappointment and hurt was how important it was for me to keep my son balanced. I put him before me.

What eventually made me a happier person was to focus on keeping him happy. To not think that he's the blame for this horrible travesty that has befallen us. Not placing blame, but I began to realize that his dad was not who I thought he was. That was a huge disappointment for me.

On the other hand, it helped me become stronger. My life began to dismantle at age 30 when we separated, but quite frankly it was probably the best thing that could have happened to me. As horrible as it was, I was a spoiled brat and the demise of my marriage turned me into a better person.

It made me become much more spiritual. I realized that to get through these hard times I had to depend on prayer, because it wasn't easy. I am a testament to the fact that prayer works, but I am not a person who goes to church. I am not religious in that way, however, I am highly spiritual and I believe in God.

Then I had to work on myself. I had to become a better, nicer, less selfish, more compassionate, and caring person. I wasn't an awful, horrible person before that, but it made me work at being better.

I had to become independent. I'm from the south and I'm a Southern belle. I was raised to believe that a man is supposed to take care of you because that's his job. Well, I had to take care of my son and me. Gaining my independence was kind of a miracle. Two of the best compliments I ever received in my life came from a friend of my mother's in my hometown, and one of my uncles. They both said to me, "I'm so proud of you. You are surviving and doing a good job and I never thought that would happen." Those words gave me even more strength and I thought to myself, I can do this.

I realized that I have one person in this world to rely on and that's me. I am an only child so I had the support of my parents during this time, but I began to understand that I needed to do it myself. As wonderful as your parents are and as supportive as they are, they too can be a little controlling. If they're going to give support they want it to be their way, not your way. I had to gently let them know that this has got to be my way; I can't do it your way.

As a married woman I was totally devoted to my husband and I didn't nurture friendships as much as I should have. I found that when all this stuff falls down, your friends are still there and that man is gone. I will never commit myself that emotionally to a man again. It's not that I won't love him and nurture the relationship, but I will *always* keep my girlfriends in my life. I will continue to do things with them because I enjoy their company and I've learned that if the next relationship falls by the wayside, my girlfriends are still going to be there.

I was married at a young age and I did a lot of dating after I was separated and divorced. At first, I thought you only go out when you have a date, but I had to learn to make plans and do things with girlfriends, then come home.

Managing Your Thoughts

I've learned to live here by myself and I quite like it. I don't think I ever want to get married again. No, I know I don't. I don't even want to live with someone. I am hoping and praying that when I get into another relationship it will be with someone who feels the same way, so that we can live apart, yet come together and have a wonderful life.

The Forgiveness Factor

DINA

The biggest lesson I learned about managing my thoughts after my divorce was the forgiveness factor. Immediately, once I realized we were on the road to divorce I forgave him. No matter the cause or who I thought was right or wrong, I did it early, fast and it turned out to be the best thing for me to get through the situation. It meant there was no bitterness for me toward him. Right away, it freed me although it didn't take care of the financial worries I had and all that. It lifted an emotional burden off me, however, and freed me right away.

I decided I wasn't going to spend my life chasing him down for child support or anything else. I'll go through the motions of getting stuff like that, but I am not going to spend my life talking about, you're no kind of dad. Or you're no kind of husband because you did this or whatever. Right away I freed myself of it, and said, "I forgive you."

If we're going to divorce it's not just a settling of our marriage, it's settling the emotional ties that go with it, too. I needed to let it go and forgive because I didn't want to be hanging onto anger, resentment and bitterness after the marriage was over, especially

Managing Your Thoughts

when I have a child. I wanted to show love for my child and his father.

A big part of the reason I took that route is because of my mother. My mother and father divorced when I was about four years old. My mother forgave my dad for all his craziness that I never knew about. I did not know that my mother disliked my dad until I was seventeen years old. She took the high road and never showed me any negative feelings toward my dad. It wasn't until my dad and I had a falling out that she finally came clean about it. I was upset because he had let me down by not keeping his word. She told me, "I can't stand that man, don't worry. I am not going to let him do anything to you that will hurt you." It was an eye-opening experience even though I was only a teenager. I didn't know that would help me later on in life. It made me look at the most important factor in this whole situation, my child. My mom did that for me and I can do that for my child.

So I held no ill will, no matter what his father had done and I'm telling you, he did some stuff. He wasn't there the way he should have been. He pretty much walked out of my son's life when we went overseas for two years. I took the high road, I was a mother first. I just want my son to know love. For him to believe that his father loves him although he wasn't showing it appropriately. During the two years we were living abroad I showed my son pictures of his dad so he wouldn't forget who he was and I talked about him often. I forgave so I could help my son live in love.

It also helped me get over it because I didn't join those resentment parties when my girlfriends would gather and talk about *bad dads*. Though his father sometimes belonged in that class, I didn't have that to talk about, because it wasn't a part of my life. I never focused on it. I don't care and in the end he has to answer to God for that. It's a non-issue for me.

God was my husband for those years. He provided for me and my child and helped me get through it and in the end we got over it. There is no resentment. Before I divorced, I gave everything I could to make that marriage work. By the time we got to the point of divorce I knew I had exercised everything and anything that I could. It just wasn't happening.

You need two people to make a marriage work. One can't fight if the other one isn't fighting. I walked away with a clear conscience knowing I had done all I could.

My only issue with him was his fathering. It was like you left me, please don't leave my child. He still needs a father, so could you please step up and be more of a dad? That never happened the way I hoped it would and he's never been the dad that he should have, but our son got through it.

It wasn't until now that he's 21 that he realizes the kind of father he has, unfortunately. He was blind to it during his childhood. So, it worked out, and that's all I can say. It worked out for all three of us because when my son was growing up he thought his father was the world. I knew better, but I never told him. I let him believe whatever he wanted to about his father.

He had a rude awakening when he went off to college. He had to interact with his dad at an adult level when the college was sending the bills and stuff to him now. He had to follow up with his dad, 'you said you were going to do this? Where is it?' Now the blinders are coming off. That it was always me behind the scenes coming through. He finally realized what had been going on all along and how I protected him from that.

I tell him, "It's OK, your dad's going to want to come back in your life later on and he's going to regret it. When he gets older he's going to wish that he hadn't missed these times." This is his only child and he is my only child, too. Even though I have had the struggle of being his primary financial and emotional support, I get the best part of it. I get to see all the good stuff because I got to watch him grow up. I think about his father, man you are such a loss. You don't know what you're missing. All he sees is the money, but who his son really is and the person he is inside, you can only know from spending those small moments with him.

After your child grows and takes the blinders off, they appreciate you, if you've done the right thing. My son is always posting stuff about me on Facebook. On his 21st birthday, he wrote on his wall: My MOM is the *Greatest Mom Ever!* I could not be the man I am today without my mother and on and on. I was so moved. I know his father saw it. That was redeeming. It made me happier. Exactly, it made me happier after! It was priceless.

Chapter Three

DOING GOOD FOR OTHERS

Doing what makes them feel useful and good inside was important to almost every woman interviewed. In the immediate aftermath it helped them find a place to show all that extra love that was leftover when they no longer had a man in their lives. For many of the mothers, it was their children. For others it was other people's children and for one mom that child became her very own.

Others showed love to organizations or animals, during the breakup or years later once they felt they had something to contribute. Overall over three-quarters of the women felt doing good for others without an expectation of anything in return made a difference to their happiness.

Shines From Within

ALEXIS

By doing things for others, you're doing for yourself. I went through a yearlong study of a book called, *A Course in Miracles*, which was about recognition of the light in the world as opposed to the focus on the darkness. My counselor was remote so we held sessions over the phone for a year by reading chapter after chapter and exploring our lives.

I came to the realization that we shine the light on ourselves. The spotlight doesn't shine from outside, it comes from within. It was a spiritual awakening to know that a person can be one with others without overcoming them. It was about listening and hearing other's life stories. I think that's what connects us, acknowledging that we all come from God and return to God. And we all return to God alone, even if we're a couple during life.

Assisting and Supporting

KIM

I help other single moms. Over these years I have reached out in many ways. Currently I am helping someone who lives with me and has a three-year old daughter. I have known her for some time and I'm not trying to hold anything over her or expect anything from her. It's about assisting and supporting her and helping with things that she does not know. I talk with her so she that she's able to go out on her own and make it. Sometimes, I go out of my way.

Other times it's just talking with them. People can be lacking a hug, or just hearing "it's going to bc ok," and I can explain why.

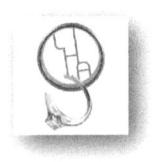

Unconditionally

KANDI

I am the kind of person that does things for others. I am always the person at the office planning someone's party. I give without thinking about what might be in it for me. For years, I have done this and years later people have done really unexpected things for me.

Once my sister-in-law and brother helped me out when I was experiencing a rough time. She said, I'm happy to be able to do this for you because you did *this* for me. I had totally forgotten about the assistance that I'd given them back when things were hard for me! I do things unconditionally and try to pay my blessings forward. God has started to bless me now for the things I did back then.

Be of Service

TAMRA

It is extraordinarily important for me to do things that really make me feel good, that make me happy. Often that is service, being able to extend myself in a way that makes me feel useful. I can't say that I ever do things for others expecting something in return. I don't expect anything from them, necessarily, but I do expect something from me.

I make choices to do things that make me feel good. For instance, I work in a yoga studio and volunteer my time. I love being around people who practice yoga. They're more mindful about their lives and they are just wonderful people. I clean the floors and the toilets. I wash the clothes, mop the floors and I love it. I love being there, it feels good, and I feel good. It's an incredible opportunity to serve and I get a great deal from it in return.

I also coach young women and it just adds to my happiness. I feel like I'm using my life in a way that makes sense for me. One of the things that my ex used to say after we had a son with Down's Syndrome was, "you're too old to be trying to follow your dreams." I thought, 'oh, it's time for him to go.'

Living Happier After

What I learned is that every day I want to do something for my dream. It very well might have something to do with someone else, but it always makes my heart feel better.

Fostering

SHEREE

I became a foster parent and began to take children in and love on my children's friends who were without parents. When we moved into a new town there were these two young guys. They weren't brothers, but they had family situations where their parents had basically abandoned them and I took those boys in.

I had so much love left over when I found myself in the midst of divorce. I had all this extra 'stuff,' which started the fostering phase of my life. Because of my inability to be focused on another relationship, I didn't want to branch out. I didn't even want to think about dating another man. I needed to direct all this love somewhere so I began to love on children.

For my kid's friends, my house became the neighborhood house with the trampolines, the toys and everything. Children were there 24/7 and it was a safe place for them to hang out. I began with those first two foster kids and I have been fostering ever since.

Book Club

CYNTHIA

It started out serendipitously I guess, because I'm an avid reader. I had a couple of girlfriends and when I told them I was finished crying and talking about my ex and all of that stuff, I said, "Let's do something productive. Let's improve ourselves." So we started going to museums and other cultural events in our city. Then I decided we should start a book club. That book club is still meeting almost twenty years later. It grew from me and those two good girlfriends to about twenty women. We're married, singles, all of that. Some relationships have ended and some have begun in the twenty-year span of time we've been together.

I also poured myself into my child in a very healthy way. I was filling in the space that his father left when he was out of the country for a couple of years. It created such a strong bond between the two of us that I think even now his father looks at it with some envy. While he and our son have a good relationship with mutual admiration, they love each other and all of that, he realizes that there are things about, we call him 'the boy' that he just doesn't know because I've put in the time, and he hasn't.

Kept the Name

DINA

My biggest focus was my son. He was it, and I wanted to make sure he got through everything OK. Although he was too young to know everything that was going on, I wanted to make sure he was least impacted by the situation.

One of the things my mother advised me on was keeping my ex's last name after the divorce. She was like, "I kept your daddy's name for y'all. You should do it for him." I think that's the only dilemma I have all these years after having the divorce, is having his name. Twenty-two years later and I still have his name! But I did it for my kid.

My mom said that I should do it because of the outside world. What if my mother had a different name than the rest of us, especially back in the 70's? People would start questioning her. She said, "I kept your dad's name for you guys since y'all had his name." She told me she thought it would be easier for my son as a child, if he and his mother had the same name, so I kept his dad's name.

When he hit teenage years, he started asking me about that, "Ma, why do you still have dad's name?"

I told him, "I did it for you."

"Oh, now it doesn't matter to me. If you want to change your name back, you can change your name," he said.

Once he was older, he figured it out, but when he was a kid I think it was better for him, because most of his friend's parents were married. They all had the same name as their parents so I think it made it easier for him because he wasn't the odd man out.

What Single Women Do

ADRIENNE

For me it was my son, too. He is my only child and he and his dad were really close. He was upset that his dad wasn't there every night, he was devastated by it.

I made a decision that I wasn't going to change his life any further until I figured things out. I didn't know what to do. At first I didn't know if I should move, or if I should continue paying the mortgage. My husband knew that I could financially pay the mortgage on my own so he stopped paying it. I made up my mind that I was going to stay and pay that mortgage and maintain that house.

My ex was mad at me because I was determined to continue to be separated.

I stayed home every night with my son for about six months because he was the type of kid who needed his rest. He was on a schedule and went to bed every night around 8:30. I was determined that I wasn't going to rip and run the streets and have him worry about his dad and his mom not being there. Those rare times when I did hang out I would take him over to my mom's house about 10 or 15 minutes away.

I have to tell you though, I was bored to death at night. I'm in the house by myself for the first time as the only adult and my son is in bed at 8:30. Do you know what a long night that is? I was like, what the heck am I going to do for the rest of the night? I was frustrated because I didn't know what to do with myself.

I happened to mention it to a friend at work. We didn't normally have deep, personal conversations, but she had been single for a long time. She told me I needed to do what all single women do. I told her that when I was single the last time, I was a lot younger. When I was a young single woman my choices were different. I didn't know what to do at this age. Now I had a son and I was over forty years old. She told me, you get a couple of movies, you get a little wine, you get a book, you talk on the phone with a girlfriend or you call a couple of relatives. She was right.

So I would start my little *second act* of the night. I would either watch TV, get a couple of movies or read a book. These were things that I never had to do before because my ex was always around. We were always either taking our son out or doing things. It paid off, however, because while my son did blame me for the separation, he knew I never left him.

I sacrificed my happiness for six months or so to get him to the point where he felt we didn't both abandon him. It was really hard for me, but I had to do it.

He's My Son

CAMILLE

My ex-husband and I were still dating at the time and we hadn't discussed marriage or anything. His two-year old son from a previous relationship, AJ, came to visit for the weekend. I was active duty military. At the end of the visit on Sunday night, we took him home and the people at the house opened the door and told us that AJ's mom didn't live there anymore. We were like, what? What do you mean? We took him to my future mother-in-law's house. She told us, you guys have to take him.

I was a single mom to a son already. AJ didn't have anything, a couple of pull-ups, the dirty outfits in the bag from the weekend and what he had on. I couldn't leave him there, so he stayed at my house with me, his dad and my son. A week later, his mom called and told us to keep him and that was it. She disappeared out of the picture. Soon after AJ got really sick and his mom had all of his medical cards and documentation. I looked at him and I loved him. All he needed was someone to love him and I was in love with his dad so I married him. Then AJ was able to get benefits.

Throughout the years, whenever my ex and I would break up he would always leave AJ with me, my son and our daughter, who was born after we married. One time he took him when he left me and AJ got really mad. My mother-in-law called me and said, "He wants to come home to his mommy!"

When I ended the marriage the court awarded me custody of AJ. I have physical custody of my stepson and we share joint legal custody. AJ came to live with me when he was two years and he just turned seventeen. He'll graduate from high school next year. I am the only mom he knows and his dad doesn't exist in his life. It's just me loving him. It was great but it was hard.

His mother showed up once, told him a bunch of lies and broke his heart. I was there to pick him up, mend him and let him know that he has a mommy. I explained to him that he has a mother who gave birth to him, but I'm your mommy because I love you regardless of what's going on. He's been a good boy and I love him.

I don't do anything with the expectation of getting something in return. That's how a lot of people get their feelings hurt and get devastated. They have high expectations of getting something back and then when it doesn't happen, they get hurt. If you do something from the kindness of your heart, the blessings flow, they come to you.

I love him like he's my own. Having him with me after the divorce has made me happier after. I don't do the whole stepson thing with him. He's my son and I treat him exactly like the other two, as if I gave birth to him. From two until seventeen, now he's *my* son.

Little Things

MELISSA

It was hard for me to do things for others immediately after we separated because I was upset. I was doing everything myself and I could not count on my ex to show up to pick up the kids or keep his word in any way. It was hard to manage or control my emotions.

I signed my oldest son up for a service event in our community. It was a way to keep him occupied on the weekends. The event also included a mother-son dance so I had to practice and work with him for several months to prepare for the performance.

A couple of weeks after the event, my younger son became seriously ill and was admitted to the hospital. The affliction was not life-threatening, but it was very serious. This caused me to rely on my faith in God like never before. It was a long period of recovery, with home nurses and very strong medications. I am thankful and grateful for his recovery, but during that time I could only do small things for other people.

While my son was in the hospital I spent time in the chapel. I prayed for his recovery and for my strength. I had the opportunity to interact with other parents praying for the same things for their families. Many of them had children with cancer or other life-threatening illnesses. I began to look at my situation in a new light and I saw that I had blessings coming from multiple sources. I knew I needed to start being more positive, to start expecting and acting as if everything were going to work out just as I planned. Or even better.

I began to try to do one nice thing for somebody every day, whether they knew me or not. When I arrived at the office building in the morning, if I saw someone who was a few steps behind me I would hold the elevator door for them for a second. They wouldn't even know that I was holding it until they would open the door from the parking lot and I would say, "Are you going up?" That is the kind of thing I tried to do to put a little bit of positivity in someone else's day. It always helped make my day better, too.

I also tried to be more thoughtful of people. I did little things like sending someone a card. That's something that was done for me when I just couldn't get through a service at church. Everything just upset me. Everything made me cry. The songs made me cry. Seeing two people together, husband and wife in church, made me cry. I had to go though, because I had two sons and church is what we do on Sunday.

We have a part of the service where people testify. They stand and ask the church for prayer, or tell about a great thing that happened or whatever. Sometimes folks would say, it's my 20th wedding anniversary to my lovely bride and we're so happy. Goodness freakin' gracious! I used to have to bring tissues with me every Sunday. During that time one of my fellow members sent me a card. I was so touched because I felt like somebody sees me and somebody notices and I started trying to be that person for somebody else.

Good with My Dogs

KATHY

I love giving to others. I always have and that's why I stay broke. Not just in the monetary way. I'll go out of my way for someone that I care for. I have found myself going out of my way for perfect strangers because they had a good vibe. But I don't expect anything in return because that's just not the way to be and that's the way I was raised.

Those three years that I was going through all that with my ex, I was at work trying to help interns find jobs. I gave references, trained them and tried to send them in the right direction. I helped a family here in my community and even offered to let them come here and stay. Helping somebody else takes your mind off things and makes you feel good.

Animals are my joy! Dogs are the most interesting animals to me. When I was seven years old, my father bought a farm and we moved from NYC to a very rural area. City life was cool, but when I got here I had freedom, I could go wherever in the heck I wanted to and I didn't have to worry about a thing. We had a neighborhood full of moms and dads and everybody watched out for each other, for the kids and the animals. If somebody's animal got loose they'd call them up and say, 'did you know your cow is out?' I have always been around animals.

During that tough three year period after my marriage broke up, I got three dogs. All three had personalities of their own and they gave me more pleasure than the world. I spoil my dogs ridiculously and they seem to think they're human.

My animals have definitely helped to make me happier after. They're really not that different from humans. You can call me crazy, no problem.

An Unlikely Friend

TERESA

As part of my settlement from my husband I received $3,000 per month for a year. I was having a hard time getting over everything so my ex's sister told me I needed to meet his last wife, because she went through exactly what I was going through. She was more than willing to do that.

The first time we met at a Sunday brunch event, we spent ten hours drinking champagne and talking. It was an eye-opener! It was like a weight was taken off my shoulders. At first I couldn't figure any of it out, but once I spoke with her things started making sense.

We met many times and I met her kids from her first marriage (not my ex's). They came over for Thanksgiving with my family and friends. I wanted to replace every event that I'd gone through with my husband, with a good event and good people around.

When I received the last payment of $3,000 from my ex, I gave her and both her children, who were in their twenties, $1,000 each. I figured she saved me thousands of dollars in therapy fees. I told the kids, "I know what punishment you went through living with him." He would croak if he knew that's what I did with the money, but it was the right thing to do.

Once I Had Something to Say

Peggy

Years later, after I got confidence in myself, I had something to say and felt I could help someone I reached out to help others. That happened after I got my education. I dropped out of school in the ninth grade and never did make it to high school. But I got my GED, went to undergrad and then went to law school.

I started counseling what they called at risk youth. Kids who had done more or less the same kind of things I did when I was younger. There was a guidance center where I used to volunteer. The courts ordered young people to this program to help them get life skills, parenting skills, their GED and to plan their life and try to get something together. I used to counsel them, to help them find a focus and a reason to know that they can get out of the *hood* if they choose to.

It turned out to be better for me than for some of them because that was part of my way of trying to prove that I had done it and that I really was living happier after. I was a textbook at-risk youth back in the day, but I got out of the hood, an abusive marriage and more. If I could do it, so could they.

    I started by introducing myself. Now this program had counselors and people who had degrees in this, they had read all the books and were very educated. But I had actually been where these kids were and had made it out of there. Within the first five minutes that I started talking, they had a lot of respect for me. Many of them listened and I was able to help quite a few kids. It helped me just as much, probably more.

Chapter Four

NURTURING RELATIONSHIPS

Nurturing relationships with family and friends including forgiveness was an important part of the lives of each woman. Everyone has issues and problems in their lives in addition to the huge relationship problem of divorce.

Women that are living happier after don't focus on revenge or getting people back for what they perceive has been done to them. Nor do they incessantly beat up themselves for their words or actions from the past. They looked realistically at their lives and reached out to secure help when they needed it, whether social, psychological or spiritual.

A variety of perspectives lead to a similar conclusion: relationships matter to your happiness.

Forgiving the Abuse

KANDI

It took me a while to begin forgiving him for the abuse. Even though it wasn't physical, it was mental, abuse is abuse. I recognized it for what it was. It took me a while to get to that point, but now that I'm there, I feel sorry for him. He's not at the point of forgiveness. I can tell he still doesn't forgive me. He still has hatred in his heart.

Let me give you an example of what I had to deal with. First of all, as long as we were together I always had a job. We were a two income family. He never took care of me. So on one occasion we go to Sears to buy a washer and dryer and as we're sitting in the car before going into the store he tells me, "You are not to speak. I do all the talking. You are with me, but you are not to speak."

We go in the store, but this time I opened my mouth to say something. When we got back to the car, that's all we talked about all the way home. He would not speak to me for several days. Shaking his head and saying, "I can't believe it." What's worse, I could have been the one paying for the appliances. I had lost my personality, my identity. I lost who I was and I became the person he wanted me to be.

Nurturing Relationships

Toward the end of the relationship I needed a car because my car broke down. He had a van that we financed through a loan at my credit union. Every two weeks the payment for the van came out of my paycheck. I wanted a new car because my car had broken down and it was an older car.

"I work every day, I can't get a car?"

"No, you can't get a car."

This time I woke up. I rented a car. He said "no, me and your father are going to fix your car." (My father was a mechanic.)

"Whoa, wait a minute. Why can't I have a new car?"

His money was separate. We couldn't have a joint account for paying bills and stuff. Oh no, no, no, no, no. No, you do yours and I'll do mine. Except for when mine was his. This time I went to a dealership and purchased a brand new Toyota Camry. His brother told him I had purchased a new red car. He went off. He wasn't paying the car note or anything, but *he* went off. I had finally done something for myself. He was feeling threatened. His business was going down and I was moving up at the company where I worked. I didn't realize this at the time, but I know now. The more money I made, the more threatened he became, and the more abusive he became. I started slowly praying and getting myself together; to get my strength together to do what I had to do. And I did it.

I am not there yet, to a totally nurturing, forgiving relationship, but I am getting there. I am gaining a strong relationship with God. That means more to me than anything. That material stuff, doesn't mean anything. I had a Mercedes; I had two homes, now I have peace of mind. That other stuff doesn't matter. You don't know where I've been. I have peace of mind. Once you get peace of mind that crap is not going to mean anything.

I'm fine. I'm happy. I'm OK. I don't have somebody looking down on me telling me you ain't shit. You ain't *gonna* never be nothing; constantly telling me, that everything is my fault. Not loving me and caring for me and being there for me. It took me a while to love me, to be OK with me, to be with me; and that being alone with me is OK. It took me a while to get to that place. But I am there!

He comes by to see the kids and I know it blows his mind that I have my own things. I know it bothers him to watch me because he told me that I would never make it without him. I am so, so blessed and so thankful to God that he has taken me out of that situation. I pray for women that stay. I pray for them.

Daily Conversations with God

KATHY

As far as the relationship with myself, I'm still working on that one. I haven't quite figured out me, yet. I think basically that is my problem. I think I know me, but then I really don't. I know me enough to have left an abusive relationship. I was having thoughts of killing him. I bought a set of cast iron pots and I was going to crush his skull in. I prayed to God not to let me do that. I didn't want the kids to have their mom in jail.

I reported him doing what he did, but the police here didn't think that it was important enough to write a report on, so I developed a really great relationship with God. That's my strength. To help me get through, we have daily conversations. It helps me with my family.

My mother has Alzheimer's and my dad's hitting 90 years old. He still has all his faculties, but he's kind of letting mom wear him down. He loves her so I just try to roll and go with the flow. I have a son who has schizophrenia and is in a mental institution. My daughter is doing well, but I worry about her because of her relationships. I don't want her to end up like me. She seems to be taking a slightly different path with men though. I am glad because like me she is a good-natured, kind hearted person. I am close to my family and my friends, although I think I am closer to my friends than I am to my family.

As far as my ex is concerned, I cannot see or talk to him. I forgave him for what he did a long time ago. I had to for my sanity. If you hold onto a lot of rage and hate, you'll discover that it will pretty much tear you up inside, and that's not cool. I experienced that. So I let it go. I forgive him. I'm happy that I don't see him.

He Was a Lost Soul

PEGGY

I have two things to share from a nurturing relationships perspective, forgiveness and faith. As far as my estranged spouse; God bless and rest his soul. I have to admit that I never said bad things to my son about his dad. I knew, unfortunately that he would find out about the bad things as he grew older and grew into a man. I'm glad I didn't badmouth him myself. Later in his life he got really sick. He died, some would say because of the life he lived and that's why it happened.

He got married again and his second wife had to take care of him through his sickness. I used to tell my girlfriends that I was glad that I was not with him. If I had to take care of him at that time, I probably would have ruined my chances at getting into heaven because I would have been crushing a glass and feeding it to him every day, because of the way he treated me. That's the way I felt.

As I got better and more grounded in the foundation of my faith, I was able to able to actually forgive the man for all that he had done. I stopped repeating that joke about feeding him glass that would have messed up my chance at heaven. I know the reason he treated me the way he did is because he was a lost soul. OK? He was an intelligent man. The fact that I forgave him made it better for me. I was able to win my fight to get my spirit right and have my faith grow. I'm saved now, I wouldn't have been able to get that way.

Forgive and Move On

TERESA

The person I needed to forgive the most was me. I didn't know that in the beginning. People would say you need to learn how to forgive the person who hurt you. I spent a lot of time obsessing about what had been done to me. I put the blame on someone else. I would always say, why would I forgive that person? What he did was a very intentional, hateful, hurtful thing and I just couldn't get beyond that. It took so much spiritual, internal thought and time. Time doesn't heal all wounds. In time, however, through great introspection, thought, desire and concentrating on what needs to be done, you may begin the process. I had to tell myself every day and remind myself sometimes on an hourly basis what I had to do. I couldn't forgive myself immediately. It took months and months.

At first I didn't get it. It didn't make a difference what my ex did; it was me I had to forgive. I made decisions that weren't good for me. I allowed things to happen to my family that were wrong. What happened to me that I let that happen? It wasn't until I got on my knees that I actually realized it's about forgiving me, loving me and finding acceptance and worth in myself. That's really how I got beyond it. Boy, it took a long time. Finally, I don't know if there's a pivotal time when something really happens, but I had this aha moment when I realized I had to forgive myself.

    I ran into my ex at an event, which I knew would happen. As I looked at him enjoying himself, and I thought it doesn't hurt him at all that I am angry with him. I mean he's moved on. I am the one who is keeping me stuck in a very bad place. Quite honestly, I just got sick and tired of being sick and tired. I was sick of myself and who I was. I thought, psssfff, just give it up. Give it up and move on. And it just all disappeared. And that's how it happened.

Forgive Me and Him

Melissa

Like some other people, I had to forgive me. I really did some stupid stuff. After it was over, I never second guessed myself. I didn't question whether our relationship would have made it if we made different choices. It didn't matter because I knew it still wouldn't have worked out. After seventeen years of him cheating and my inappropriate reactions to the pain, they truly killed the love in our marriage. I really do believe that the person who cheats, cheats because of what's in them. Since I was the one that decided the relationship was over, I knew I needed to end the "woe is me" song and focus on the positive outcomes from the relationship.

I have a lot to be happy about. I was married for nineteen years. I've become a *rock star* in terms of things that are important as a person and a mother. My children are intelligent and respectful. My word means something and can be depended on no matter what. I've established traditions, things that my children have as a part of growing up. I built memories and created experiences that have carried my family's history and legacy on to the next generation. I'm really, really proud of that.

I'm in awe of the fact that I've had these opportunities in my life. I know that there are people who might have wanted to have kids and didn't have kids. Or maybe they wanted to get married and they never got married. We had some good times you know, it wasn't all bad.

So the first thing I had to do was forgive myself for the mistakes that I made. I also had to forgive myself for having such a big mouth. I think my talking so much definitely had something to do with the bad things in the relationship between my ex and me. I had to forgive him for not being true to me, not cherishing me, and not loving me at the end the way he had in the beginning. I had the textbook experience, he did everything to get me and then only what was necessary to keep me. I remember my thoughts then, "if I just accomplish this, if I just do one more thing he'll love me the way he loved me in the beginning of our relationship."

I finally realized, 'that man ain't ever trying to love you again like that!' I was just tired of the bell curve, one day way up and the next day disaster. So I forgave me. I forgave him. The only person I haven't forgiven is one of his friends. That's because I feel like I'll get there when I get there. The people who knew what was going on and yet smiled in my face, that's hard for me to forgive. That's someplace I need to get to. I'm not there yet. But you know, the Lord still has me on this earth so I am going to keep moving on.

Forgiving him, and most of all forgiving me were critical to me being able to move forward. I'm one of those people who will misspeak and say something to somebody. Then when I see them again I say, "I'm so sorry I said that."

And they go, "You said what?"

It was like, they didn't even think about it. So one of the things that I started doing, at the end of the day, I leave it alone. Ask the Lord for forgiveness and let it go. If the person doesn't say anything to me it was probably a blip in the fabric of their day. I realized I have to nurture a relationship with myself from a forgiveness

Nurturing Relationships

perspective so I don't let negative self-talk and fear take up space up in my life. You know, I only get 24 hours in a day, why am I going to spend three minutes worrying about something that might not ever happen?

My relationships are critical. I got into God. I always went to church, but my relationship with the Lord Jesus is totally different. I understand now when preachers say you got to be broken in order to be built up and become stronger. Man, whoa, ain't nothing like having your relationship break down, especially when you've done everything to keep it going. My relationship with God is the foundation of what I stood on when I couldn't stand by myself.

He's Moved On

ALEXIS

I was the one that left the relationship; the pain I was experiencing was inside of me more than anything that he actually did. There were some crazy things. He had a DWI and wrecked his car. There was an instance where he was flirting with somebody and left his phone on after talking to me. He stayed out all night a couple of times. I was alone way before we broke up. He had a different lifestyle. He was much younger, into the party scene and wanted to go out dancing after work, I'm not into that. We had kind of separate lives so I'm not sure that there was anything to forgive necessarily.

I almost didn't feel it was a marked transition into this state of euphoria. It was more of a gradual settling into my own personal rhythm. We all have kind of a cycle to our lives. When people disrupt your life, they interfere with your pace and your sense of being in the world. That's spiritually draining. I came to understand that he had a different pattern to his life and a different rhythm to it, one that I couldn't adapt to. It's kind of like a dance and we weren't on the same step. I found that I could dance alone and feel quite good about it.

My Kids Forgiveness

SHEREE

The most important thing I did for nurturing was to ask my kids to forgive me. My kids always showered me with Father's Day gifts because they saw mom doing the dual role thing. The kids and I were sitting around on Father's Day and we were just talking. I said I truly thank you for all the gifts and cards, but the greatest gift that I can get from you all is to ask you to forgive me for anything negative I said about your father. I told them, it's been hard, it's been rough, and I'm hurt. But I don't want everybody hurt. In order for us to be that solid family that we strive to be and for me to be whole, I have to ask you guys to forgive me for saying bad things about your daddy. As of this day, I'm not doing it. I'm not going to come against your daddy with words. I went to my kids and wiped the record clean of anything I had said and expressed out of frustration and anger. I didn't want to give them ideas on how to love or not love their daddy; how to respect him or not to respect him. So I asked them to forgive me if I had planted that seed in them.

That freed me in a lot of areas, it really did. I basically asked for forgiveness and then I bowed out. Whatever transpired between them and their dad, it wasn't because of what I said, but because of what they saw and they experienced. I had to take ownership of my hurt, my pain. I had to realize that pain was for me, not for the kids. It took me being the bigger person, the more grounded person to say "Hey, I'm weak in this area, you know. I need to ask you guys to forgive me in order to help me love y'all better." Help mom out here.

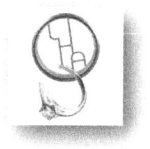

Forgiveness Is Not Needed

TAMRA

At some point forgiveness is something that is not even needed. It becomes unnecessary because every experience teaches us and helps us. It's there to move us into a greater way of being. At some point, I don't have to forgive because all I need to do is say, "thank you."

Thank you for what you did. Thank you because I needed it for my growth and my evolution. I have been exploring this principle for a while: how necessary is forgiveness? If I truly believe that everything is happening for me, and nothing is happening against me, why do I need to forgive? Everything is happening for me. I live in this sort of wide open receptive space, trusting the universe that all things are for my good, for my growth, for my evolution, for my healing and for my transformation. The people in my life are serving that. Everyone is serving that in me. And I am serving that in them. If that's the case, then no forgiveness is needed. I take a lot of deep breaths on that one because I am not completely there, but I'm there more than I've ever have been. Even if the moment feels painful, I realize it's giving me something that I need for now, because the future doesn't exist.

So for instance, in my experience with my ex, he was having an affair. Now he's never acknowledged this, or said anything out loud. When I discovered that he was having an affair, I never went to him about it. I never said anything to him, however, I immediately started saying to myself, "Thank God for this woman. Thank God for this woman who is rescuing me. This woman has come to save my life."

Whoa! I literally was able to be in deep appreciation for her. Now there were things that he did that pissed me off. He moved in with her without me meeting her, and had our child there, and that kind of stuff really stung, because I felt disrespected. It was the medicine that I had to take. Several years prior to her coming into our lives I had dreamed of this woman before she came. In the dream, I saw him talking with her somewhere, but I was afraid. She was a young Mexican woman. Even though I was with a man who said I was too old to follow my dreams and had all sorts of ideas about life that didn't fit me, I would have never left that marriage.

But because she came, I got free and now I am living my dream. Now I am living in a way that is much more conducive to whom I am. I don't have to forgive her. I thank her every time I see her. Yes, every time I see her. Now I do know her. I hug her and I tell her how much I appreciate her. She's so afraid of me. No, she really is, because she knows in her soul what went down. But I know in my soul what went down too, and I am grateful for her. I just am. I really am. I knew it in the moment, although I forgot it for a little while. But in the moment, when it was occurring, I was clear.

My Relationship with My Parents

VICKI

I can talk to you about my family. Yeah, and I can talk about my girlfriends, too. It's clear to me now that God puts people into your life for certain times. You know a lot of times people get wrapped up around the fact that when they have friendships, they change. I think that that's the way it's supposed to be.

From day one, when I knew that there were issues in my relationship, I knew that there was nobody that I could talk to. My family *loved* my ex-husband. I did not feel comfortable sharing who the real person was with them. I did not feel that they would believe me. This was something that I had to carry until the end.

I didn't disclose that there were issues until he moved out. Nobody in my family knew because I couldn't tell a soul. I'll tell you how bad it was, I would be driving to work and I would say to myself, "there is no way I can ever leave this man while my mama is alive." One day he came in the house after work, and we were having some kind of conversation when he jokingly said to me, "you'll never leave me while your mama is still alive." I thought that was very interesting because even though that was my thought process, I had never said that out loud to anybody.

The first person that I talked to was his father. I had a good relationship with his family, it was decent. I remember calling his father one day, because I felt like I could talk to him. I basically laid it on the line. I told him what the relationship was like, all the things that he had done. I didn't tell him the nitty-gritty details, but when I finished talking to him the first thing his father said, was he had to apologize to me. He said he takes the responsibility for the behavior of his son.

He said the reason is because that's exactly what he did to his wife. That's what his son saw growing up. So you might think that this is trivial, but I would stay in the kitchen half a day on Sunday. I had cooked up two or three meats, two or three vegetables, baked bread and everything. It's 5 o'clock. I'm ready to put dinner on the table, I'm ready to eat and you're going to tell me you're not hungry and walk out the door and go get some wings. His father said that is the exact same thing he used to do!

One time, early on in the marriage, I was so sick I literally could not get out of the bed. I had been sick for days. Do you know I had to call a cab and drag myself out of the bed and have the cab take me to the emergency room? His father went on to tell me that he just dropped his wife off when she went into labor with their kids and said, "Call me when you're ready to be picked up." So when I couldn't understand things before, after speaking with his father, things became clear.

I'm not saying I am perfect, in no way, but I am not doing anything to merit this type of behavior. You say you love me. You married me. When we get out in front of other people we got a *movie star* thing going on here. Behind closed doors, however, it is totally different. In front of people he treated me like a queen and when it came to children, he was doing everything he could including moving out of the bedroom to make sure that we didn't have any kids. When we went back home to visit his parents, however, somebody would make a comment, 'well when y'all going to start a family? When are y'all *gonna* give us some grandkids?'

He'd say, "I'm doing everything I can. I don't know what's wrong with…" There was nothing going on and it didn't have nothing to do with me and everything to do with him!

One Christmas Day everyone was in the living room opening gifts. He hadn't said, Merry Christmas or anything to me, nothing. When everyone is in the living room, he pulls a box out of his pocket. So, now he's going to give me my Christmas gift. I open it up, it's some diamond earrings; something fabulous for everyone to ooh and aahhh over and tell me how lucky I am and what a good man I have. I finally realized there was nothing I could do about him.

I told his father that his wife was good to put up with that, but I am not going to put up with that type of treatment. He said he completely understood and that he would support me in whatever decision that I made. I still didn't disclose anything to my family. That conversation gave me clarity, however, because I was so busy spinning in a cloud of why, why, why? When I finally disclosed things to my family and friends, they were taken by surprise.

They didn't know the circumstances. They had their natural reactions:

"Oh everybody has problems."

"Girl, you gotta stay there, you can't give up."

Even my parents said, "Marriage takes work." But what they didn't realize is that I had already been in there working. This has been going on for years. Through the separation they were very supportive. When my heart would get the best of me, they were there for me. After the divorce was final I called them up. I told my parents, I have to thank you, I said for actually breathing for me, because I know there were times when I actually couldn't breathe. You see, once they understood, they didn't push.

They eventually figured it out; they knew me well enough to know. After they heard the whole story, they saw that I had already done what I was supposed to do. I never lost a night of sleep over it. I knew from day one, once I realized something was wrong, that I had done everything that I was supposed to do and that I was charged to do. I was never going to look back and say, Oh you know I *shoulda*, or well you know I *coulda*. Never. I did it all up front before I was willing to say to him, "You know, you need to get up outta here."

It was My Mom

DINA

I relied on girlfriends during that time, but my biggest friend was my mother. During that time she really helped me get through it.

I didn't know I had taken the steps to heal until 30 days after we split up for good. My mother just called me out of the blue one Saturday. She said, "How are you feeling?"

I said, "Ma, I'm fine."

You know, I thought she was just, you know asking, hey how you doing, but she wasn't really asking that. She was like, "No, how do you feel?"

I said, "I feel good. I'm doing this today. I got a lot planned for today and I'm going out tonight"

And she said, "Life goes on, huh?"

I said, "What do you mean?"

She said, "How do you feel about your divorce?"

I said I hadn't really thought about it.

Then she was like, "Are you stressed today?"

I said no.

She was like. "So how do you feel?"

I thought about it and I said, "Relieved. Believe or not, relieved."

She said, "Then you made the right decision. That's all I wanted to know. I knew you would get to this place."

I hadn't even realized that I had gotten there. If she hadn't shown me I wouldn't have known. She saw it in me. She was just waiting and waiting for me, and then she was like, you're there. You're OK. You made the right decision. You're not sitting around having a pity party. You're not saying maybe we can make it work. Maybe I should be trying to get back with him. You're not focused on what was. You're sitting there making plans for the future. You're going on, creating a life, a new future, a new way of life, a new hope. You know, I hadn't realized that.

She told me, "That shows you made the right decision. Usually when you're still focusing on yesterday, or what could have been, or maybe if you had done something different or whatever, then you haven't moved on and you haven't let it go." She was saying the fact that you have plans to do this and this, tells me you made the right decision for you.

Her acknowledgement meant that I was better than I thought I was. You know what I mean? At the time, you're so into the situation, you don't see it. But she was on the outside, looking in. It was just confirmation that see, you survived, and you will continue to do that. You're going to be OK. It was just that confirmation, it's going to be alright. Now, it may not be easy, but it's going to be alright.

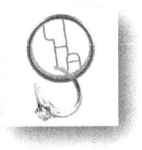

Nurtured My Son

LISA

When this whole thing happened everyone is like what are you going to do? You don't have any family in this area, how are you going to get by? How are you going to have a life? I was in my thirties when I got divorced. My parents are about 300 miles away and my brothers are about 100 miles away, so we didn't see them day-in and day-out. I believe you can make family from anyone. All my friends in the area became like family to me. I took the opportunity to make my friends even closer than they already were. Just to see them. I spent a lot of time with my friends and my family.

The most important person I got close to was my son. I thought I'd take that time to really get closer to him and be with him all the time. Every moment when I wasn't working we were always together. Just doing stuff, fun stuff. It was great; we did so much together. We're still really close, but gosh, back then it was the baby jogger all the time, going to the kiddie pool, hanging out. I taught him how to ride a bike. I'd run next to him while he'd ride his bike. We biked and ran every day. We went fishing. I have two brothers so I'm kind of a tomboy, I really like to be outside. So it was good to have a boy. My own little Bam-Bam, banging around.

We had a lot of fun together, and I never felt like I missed anything because I was older. I was really pretty stable. Except for the time when I wasn't with my son. Every other weekend and every Wednesday he was with his dad. That's when I did stuff with my friends. On my time off, I just decided to take advantage of the moment and just try to live in the moment and not feel bad about anything.

Forgiveness is part of what I learned through counseling, from Al-Anon and everything. I was so angry; I was just so mad that it didn't work out. I was really sad for a long time. So I had to forgive him. I realized not everybody has the same way of dealing with life. Everyone doesn't think like you. Everyone is different. When I see him, we hug each other. Through the whole forgiveness thing I ended up on the other side, having a lot of empathy for him. I mean there are parts where I get really mad because sometimes he doesn't pay child support. He makes me angry because he thinks that everyone should be helping him all the time. He's 53 and he still thinks that everyone needs to help him, like he's 15 because he's had a *hard time*. I have to get a grip and tell myself, that's just the way he is. He is not going to change.

Release

CAROLINE

I felt guilty because I wanted to be a better mother to my son. I became a much better mother once he entered middle school and up to now that he has graduated college and is a working adult, than when he was younger. I didn't do as much as I would have liked to have done with him. The saving grace for me was when I talked to him candidly about the time I spent with him, he said "I'm glad you didn't do more than you did 'cause it's no telling how I would have turned out. You would have smothered me."

I have had to work on it because I've been told that you really shouldn't go through life feeling guilty. So I've got to release that guilt because he's turned out wonderfully. He's the light of my life.

Nurtured My Kids

CAMILLE

I had a different perspective. I grew up in the Deep South in an environment with a lot of physical and emotional abuse. When I was growing up and I heard people say negative things to me, like you're never going to be nothing, I would always say, I'm going to be somebody. I would always take it and flip it.

When I was about seventeen or eighteen years old, they told me I couldn't have kids. Then when I was twenty, I got pregnant with my son. I had a lot of problems and pain and was told that I probably wouldn't carry to term. I prayed and prayed throughout the pregnancy. I had my son and I promised myself that I would always love my kids. Growing up I never heard the words, *I love you*. My kids and I tell each other we love each other all the time. We don't say goodbye at the end of a conversation. We say talk to you later because goodbye is like a finale. So we don't do that.

She Got Me Outta that Funk

Adrienne

I think my relationship with most of my girlfriends did not improve. I lost a couple of friends because they thought that I should give my marriage another chance. When you don't tell people what's wrong in your marriage all along they don't really understand when all of a sudden you've broken up. My real friends understood that this was personal. It wasn't up to them to have any information about what was going on in my personal life. Even with my family, everyone kind of treated me a little different. Like she must be crazy. What is wrong with her? Separating and possibly getting a divorce from this guy she's been with forever, who adores his son?

The relationship that blossomed was with my cousin, my 28-year-old second cousin. She's my first cousin's daughter. We had always been close. One time she called me and said, "Come to New York City this weekend." We hung out. We talked. When she came to the town where we lived, she'd go to dinner with us, my son and me. She literally was the best friend I could have ever asked for. Not because she let me wallow in self-pity. She was young, she wasn't married and her head was in a different place. She was about doing all she could to make me have fun whenever I could. It turned into the best relationship with any relative I ever had. Five years later she got married, she has a baby now, and so the relationship has changed. It caught me off guard at the time. If anyone would have told me that a 28-year-old would be the person to get me out of that funk, I would never have guessed that it would have been her.

My Friends and the Word

CYNTHIA

You know how when you're married you give up doing some things you used to do with your girls, right? After the breakup you have all this 'time' on your hands. Once you get past the 'I can't believe this happened to me' point, you get to the place where you can actually start doing stuff! That was really nice. I really enjoyed that part. It was important to reconnect with the stuff, and the people that I like.

I also spent a lot of time studying the Word, my Bible and being intentional about my faith walk. I guess the relationship I was nurturing was with God in large part, because when we were married we weren't of the same faith. I sacrificed a lot of my spiritual development and time for the sake of that relationship. Once it was gone, I didn't have to worry about that anymore, so I really put more emphasis on that space than I had before.

Spiritual Experience

GRETCHEN

I found my God. I don't mean religious, religious. I am not really into that. What I mean is I found my spirituality and I found my God, my higher being. I actually found a Saint Jude, a novena, because I'm Catholic. Even though I'm not into Catholic stuff, there's something about Saint Jude that I really like. You know, help for the hopeless. That's was the thing about this one novena that I found. Believe it or not, I still say that prayer every single day as I drive into work.

One day a colleague and I were in a conference room talking about God's grace. I was telling her a little about what I had just experienced with my separation and divorce and the journey that I was on. She said to me, "You have to surrender."

I don't know how to explain this without sounding like a crazy person, but all of a sudden in the course of our conversation, her face lit up. I mean whatever wrinkles she had on her face were gone. There was this gold aura or something behind her. I stared at her, like what's happening? Then I felt this tremendous peace and warmth. I guess it was grace or something. It was just this warmth shining over me. It wasn't her. It was something through her. I was like, oh my gosh! We talk about this every once in a while when we see each other. I look at her and she says, "I know."

Chapter Five

Engaging in Activities

Doing things with new friends, old ones you have rediscovered or who were there all along. Work friends. Man friends. All types of friends doing physical, cultural and joyful things together.

Women focused on attaining goals and achieving projects. Women relishing control over their life and their love. The types of activities vary but for more than half the women surveyed, engaging in activities they loved made time fly by and was critical to living happier after their divorce.

Everybody Ain't Your Friend

KANDI

I was down for so long. It took me a minute, about a year, to come around. I wasn't keeping up my appearance. I wasn't paying attention. My ex had me thinking I was big, you know, a large woman even though I am smaller than the average woman and as a result, I wore all these big baggy clothes all the time.

I relocated to a city where one of my cousins lived after the divorce. I started going out to clubs and dances with my cousin and her friends and naturally we would meet guys. My cousin is an attractive woman, with nice features, tall and she liked to be the center of attention. If she went with me, she knew she was going to be the center of attention because of the way that I dressed.

Our grandmother and aunt lived about 200 miles away and one weekend we all drove up there to see them. There was a private party scheduled at a club there, so we had plans to go out.

I had become friends with a girl that lived across the street from me who's still my buddy today. As I told her about our plans and showed her the outfit I planned to wear, she asked me, "Why are you dressing like that?"

I said, "What?"

She took me to a different store. I found out I could wear junior sizes; I didn't know that. Pants that fit! At that time halter tops were hot. My cousin had big boobs. She told me I couldn't wear halter tops because I have small breasts. My girlfriend said, "Girl, no, you can wear halter tops! Girls with big boobs can't wear halter tops. She's got you fooled."

So now I had figured it out. Oh, the looks on their faces when I walked in that club! I had my hair done and my pants fit, for the first time! Yes, I had on a little halter top. Guys were all over me! I was not used to that. I was just used to sitting. Guys never came over to me before. I had a ball.

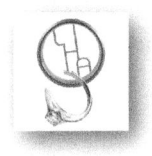

My Cheerleaders

DINA

I was in the military when we divorced. I was in an all male unit and the men in the unit would take me out to get my mind off of him. We friend-dated, I guess you could say. They would say, "Come on, let's go." They were my cheerleaders. They felt we should divorce because they watched things happen. Their opinions were, "leave him alone, you can do better than that." I didn't always agree with that logic, but that's what they thought.

They would call me up on weekends, "Hey, you want to go out? You want to go to a movie?" All my guy friends made sure I never felt lonely. They were all trying to be there. I was their girl, they had my back.

I remember one of them even said, "Here's the pen to sign your divorce papers!" I kid you not.

I said, "Y'all are silly."

They were there to make sure that I didn't fall into the trench of despair. They kept encouraging me, saying "you'll meet somebody later on." During that time when I did engage in activities, my biggest thing was hanging out with the guys. They made it easier.

Sex

TAMRA

Sex, sex, sex. Sex, sex, sex! Oh, Lord have mercy, I think every woman who has gone through divorce finds that sex starts to change in the relationship when things start going downhill.. The sex in my relationship changed right away. It was really a challenging thing. I gardened, I exercised, I rode my bike, I went to the park with my son, I went to the beach, but the thing on the top of my list was *sex*! I am a forty-year-old woman and I refuse to spend another moment of time repressing my sensuality or my sexuality for anyone.

That has been a big deal for me. I do it as often as I can. I do have a steady partner. I really hesitated when committing to this monogamous relationship. My concern was that the sex would become boring or I might not be able to get it as often as I'd like. He finally convinced me to be monogamous with him. He knows, however, if I'm going to be monogamous with him, then he has to give it up when I want it. It's just the truth. Sex is on a pretty high level of importance for me.

Living Happier After

I also eat really healthy. I take really good care of myself. I don't drink alcohol, I don't eat sugar, I don't eat flour. I prepare all my own foods. I didn't do this before, but I have started to love nurturing myself, my child and my friends; doing things that really feel loving. But number one on the list is sex!

What I Want To Do

CYNTHIA

I started going to museums and cultural events, I didn't do that before. When I was married we saw movies he wanted to see. If we went to a movie that I selected there was a gnashing of teeth. He bellyached so much so I just said, "Forget it. We'll just go to see what you want to see." So I gave up myself even for things like what movie we'd go see.

Even though we hadn't been married very long we were probably in a rut when it came to intimacy. The first relationship I had after my marriage I was like, "Oh yes, this is what I've been missing." That was a pleasant surprise.

One other thing that may seem really off the wall, but an activity I resumed after we separated, was sleeping on the right side of the bed. Before we were married we slept on the same side of the bed. When we became a couple I compromised again and let him have the side that he was comfortable on. At first I thought, how am I going to be able to sleep? We were married for two years. We met in grad school and we were together a few years before that. Once we became a couple, you know, we were a couple. Almost five years of my life sleeping with this man and then he's gone. After the divorce, I got my side of the bed back. I think I slept better as a result of returning to my own personal comfort zone. It was fantastic. I was like this is not so bad, it's alright.

I Do That

CAROLINE

During the period after my separation I used to invite a couple of girlfriends over and we'd sit around the dining room table and chat. Whatever junk I had in the freezer, we'd bake and put it on the table to eat, laugh and talk. I wanted my apartment to feel like a home. I wanted people to enjoy it. The only requirement I had was that you take your shoes off in the foyer. Other than that, put your feet up, kick back, do whatever. Just enjoy.

Now, I travel a lot. I've always travelled, but now I travel a lot more than I used to. One reason is because my mother just passed so I don't have a feeling of guilt, like I'm going off again and leaving my mom. I can just get up and go whenever I feel like it.

I love movies, theater and reading. I'm in a great book club that meets every month. I exercise a little to keep me healthy so I don't have to take cholesterol medication. Even though I'm in an apartment, I garden. Three or four years ago I decided to expand my balcony. I bought all these big planters. Every spring I plant my flowers. I enjoy watering, nurturing and taking care of them. So, yeah I do all of that.

Joy

TERESA

Everything in my life now is about joy, bringing joy to myself, my friends and my senses. It's about treating ourselves the best we possibly can.

I had to become my own caretaker. I had to understand that I was a child again and that I was raising myself. If I were raising a child, I would treat them with love, tenderness and goodness. I would want to relish them in all the good things in life. That's what I had to go back to. It's pretty primal and pretty basic, but it was so necessary.

Every morning when I wake up I say, 'Thank You. Thank you for the life that I have created." It is all focused on bringing joy and pleasure.

Laser Focused

VICKI

I was limited in what I was able to do, because I was in financial distress during that time. I was $30,000 in debt. The majority of the debt wasn't mine and that was the hard part. I was trying to figure out how to jump start my life.

My sister invited me to move in with her. So I moved out of my place and moved in with my sister to save money. Not that it was difficult to live with my sister, but it's a challenge to leave your own abode and go into someone else's. She presented a strong case. She said, "You don't even have to pay any rent, I'll pay the rent. You can stay here as long as you need to."

I wanted to purchase a home, so I set a goal for myself. I went to work every day, came home, worked out and then watched TV. I got paid every two weeks. I paid the upfront bills and with what was left over, made massive payments on the debt. Every pay period I would put every spare dime toward retiring that debt, except for $20. I would have $20 to last me from pay period to pay period, for discretionary items.

Every blue moon I would go to the movies or I would order the same thin crust Pizza Hut pizza and get a tub of ice cream on the weekend. I would lay in bed or on the couch and look at the Lifetime Channel. That was my thing. I didn't have to do anything else. I didn't have to get dressed or go out. I worked all week and there wasn't much else I could do.

I enjoyed watching Lifetime. I am remarried and my current husband calls it the 'Women's Victim Channel.' You might think, wow, is that all? You know what, it was enough.

On Sunday, I would go to early church service then I would go to the Silver Diner and have breakfast at the counter. Then I would go home and look at TV for the rest of the afternoon. I did that for a solid year.

I paid that $30,000 of debt off in one year. By then, I had secured a better job. I was starting to make more money. I had become acquainted with the person I am married to today. I became content with less based on my future goals. I proved that I could manage my resources properly and I was blessed with more.

The goal didn't include a man. I knew I wanted marriage, but I was prepared not to be married again. My girlfriends would tell me, you're not eligible to remarry until we get our first one. I knew I needed to be happy by myself. I was secure in my job. I was making enough money to not only support myself, but also to save so I could buy a house. I had a strong support system in my family and friends. If a man came along that would be great. And he did.

Music

LISA

I got in to music. I love music. Thank God for XM satellite radio! I liked just listening to the radio. Finding all the stations with music I liked. I also have this big music collection at home. Music was an outlet I could do while I was at home with my son.

Enjoy Me

ALEXIS

I got into writing lyrics. I find it an enjoyable exercise. I get a tune in my head and hours go by creating. At the end of the day, I might look at it and say, "Uh, well that was crap." The experience of creating, however, was pure joy. The finished product is a byproduct of the experience.

I tried to be in my head and enjoy the thoughts. Enjoy what flows through me. I feel more connected to the universe when I'm doing something I enjoy. I have always enjoyed the arts, and have had subscriptions to theatre and art programs. I would put off going to the movies because I'd have to go by myself. It felt like a couple thing. I find I can go to independent films, however, and be wrapped up in them. I leave without having to express a thought to someone about it. I internalize it and have my own experience with it. Once you start sharing the experience with others, sometime I feel like, "Did you see the same movie I saw?"

I Make It Happen

KATHY

Horror movies make me happy. Before I know it, hours have gone by. I'm not a girly- type movie person. I like horror flicks, science fiction, thrillers and action movies. The kinds of experiences I hope I will never be involved in, but those stories take me away. I sit here and chill. I work two jobs. Being at home is a godsend for me. Part of it is watching movies on TV to escape.

I take pride in making my home reflect me. I have an obsession with African art. If I had more money, I'd have more art in my home. Buying this sort of stuff makes you wonder about yourself. I recently found out that I have roots in Ethiopia. That is where my family started. I hope to travel there one day.

I also love to work with my hands. I am a DIY er. I like fixing and repairing things. I have about twenty projects I'm working to complete in this house. I do a little bit of this and a little bit of that. For instance, I have totally demolished my son's bedroom. I took it down to the studs. I installed the drywall myself. I put in a whole new floor. I purchased a bed and put it together myself.

When I am doing things with my hands I don't think about any- thing. I just do it. It's my stress reliever. When I finish a project I look at it and I say, "Hey, that's pretty cool and I did it myself." It makes me feel really great.

I have almost four acres of land. Every spring I plant a whole bunch of things. When it's warm I do a lot of gardening.

It doesn't take much to make me happy. The things I do like home improvement, playing with the dogs, trying to help my kids and gardening, they all intertwine. They make me feel like a better person. I'm a strong person, even though I do have my moments, but hey, who doesn't? All of it works together. I make it happen and that gives me great enjoyment.

The Club Rub

MELISSA

I've always been a voracious reader. I read a lot of self-help books, books about spirituality, life and relationships. . Information that I thought would give me some direction. I read and hours fly by.

Another thing that has always been huge for me is music. There are certain songs that I couldn't listen to immediately after my separation. They were too painful to hear. So I went back to music that I hadn't listened to in years. Rock and roll. Funky jazz. It took me to another place back when my head was stronger; when my sense of self was stronger. There was some contemporary music mixed in there, too. Sunshine Anderson's 'I Heard It All Before' was a frequent selection. As I began to feel better, Angie Stone's *My Sunshine* became my theme song.

For that first year and a half, I knew I wasn't ready to date. More important my sons were not ready for me to date. But I craved interaction with someone. Not sex, necessarily. I needed to interact in a flirtatious and somewhat sensual perspective. I found that exchange when I went dancing at the club. I named it *The Club Rub*. The crowded dance floor, the thumpin' music, the heat, you know, you've got a little wine in you and you're having a really good time.

It was important to have that type of release. I rarely gave anyone my number when my girlfriend and I went out. It was all about the dancing. Feeling desired and pursued, flirting, laughing, dancing and feeling free. It was a much needed distraction from the serious and unpleasant problems I faced on a daily basis.

Although my *Club Rub* period has ended, one habit I started during the separation continues to this day. I get up every morning and I walk. Sometimes I walk hard, like a race walker and sometimes I barely make it out the door. It is the importance of just moving. I don't like walking to be honest with you, but when I am finished, I've done something. If I don't do anything else that day, I have accomplished this something.

Release Boundaries

ADRIENNE

I always exercised really hard. I never stopped doing that during the separation and it helped. Plus, if you're crying while you're exercising hard nobody can tell. The sweat and tears mix.

After six months of staying in, I began to take occasional trips to New York City. I would hang out, go to restaurants and shop. For the first time, I did not have to report to my ex about anything and my son stayed with my mom.

During that period I dated someone that was completely different than anyone I've ever dated. He was a musician and that was a lot for fun for a while. Very different in the way he thought. It was just about the possibilities.

I've always been pretty structured. Even though I like to have fun, I always have these boundaries around what I should and should not do. During that period I let go of that a little bit and decided, "I'm having fun and I'm not going to question it." I would enjoy whatever I was doing at that particular time, which was different for me.

In The Game

KIM

I did all my activities with my family during that time. We would travel; have little mini-vacations with my sons, my parents and my brother. It was like a ritual with us, going sightseeing and going out to eat.

I made an effort to stay close. I kept myself around family and close friends. I did not want to be secluded or apart from everybody. I kept myself in the game. I refused to lose sight of what was given me as a single parent.

Control

Peggy

It sounds so small and trivial now, but when I first got divorced the fact that I was able to go to the store and use my own money to buy myself a pair of...underwear was a big joy to me. I wasn't able to do that before. I didn't even get to carry money. If I did, there was a reason for it and I'd better have a receipt.

When I was a young lady growing up the girls hand danced at parties with a male partner. I didn't know how to do that stuff because my ex-husband didn't dance and he wouldn't allow me to dance with anybody else. The fact that I could go somewhere and ask someone to dance with me; that was a wonderful thing.

Making a decision to wear a pair of pants or a skirt; all of these things may seem trivial to some people, but it was a big deal for me. I could get a massage, spend some money as I pleased, I didn't have that option before.

I like to eat sushi every week. I would never have been able to do that with him. That would have been a waste of money, because he didn't eat sushi. Now, I'm in control.

Sometimes I think because I didn't have control over the first third of my life that it's hard for me to submit as much as you need to, to find that life partner. It's kind of like I'm handicapped because of my strength. A lot of men in society today are afraid of strong women. It's unfortunate that we have to *feel* like we have to surrender anything, because we don't *have* to. Yeah, I wish I could surrender more, but right now, I just can't do it. I've got to believe that God don't make mistakes. If He got me like this, then there has got to be a man somewhere that will appreciate it.

All Along

SHEREE

I began to see myself with a whole new value. I began to tap into myself self worth. I went back to school when I was married to get a business degree because my husband had one. I was just living in his shadow. Once we separated I began to open my mind and become educated in the things that interested me. I felt free to go for it now. Before I felt ridiculed and made to feel small.

Now everything I do is for Sheree. It's not for the wrong reason or for another person. Two minutes short of a doctorate, I've worked hard for me and I'm happy about doing it.

I remember when I purchased my first home. I didn't think it was going to happen. Thinking oh God, I can't do this, my credit is bad, everything is shot, how am I going to do this? But I did and it was just phenomenal.

I felt this sense of independence because I was able to do these things. Apparently I was able to do them all along, but I thought that I couldn't. I began to take more interest in myself and my abilities. I had my independence. I was happy. At the end of the day, I didn't feel like I had to answer to anybody's standards but my own.

Chapter Six

GRATITUDE

Professing thankfulness for their lives, their spirit, their courage and God are frequent themes for this group of women. The wisdom of honoring their families and friends who stood behind and sometimes even lifted them during periods of distress.

The clarity that can only come with time brings even more grateful feelings as the years pass. Gratitude makes a big difference in becoming happier after in almost every case.

Forever Grateful

CAMILLE

It was time for me to make a change and shed everything my ex put me through. I remember giving so much of myself to everyone else, to the marriage and the kids. When I love, I love hard, so the breakup of the marriage was devastating for me.

I was blessed when I moved to this area from down south. I was recommended for a job at a company in a large metropolitan area but I didn't have a lot of experience. Well, I got the job and I was offered a $3,000 signing bonus! On top of that, when I returned home after the last interview, I received a bonus check from my current job. God was telling me it was time to make that change. He put me in a different place and I no longer had my ex in my face every day. God took me out of that situation and allowed me to grow.

When I was married I came out of the military and worked in a call center barely making ends meet. Now I have a substantial income and I'm doing it all by myself. I have learned to love me.

Some girlfriends ask me, "Aren't you tired of being single? Don't you want a man?" I tell them there's a difference between wanting and needing a man. There are two types of women in this world.

Gratitude

There are the women who need a man, physically, financially or emotionally and she'll sell her soul to have a man next to her. Then there are women like me, I don't need a man. I want a man. I want him in my life and I'm going to value him, but I don't want to lose myself in him. I'm going to keep my identity. At the same time I'm going to respect him and allow him to be a man. That's where I'm at in my life.

If someone wants to be in my life, they're going to have to go the extra mile. I will not sell *my* soul to have a man. I have a bigger man in my life, I have God. As long as I have him that's all I need at night to hold me and comfort me, to make me feel safe. Do I get lonely sometimes? Yes, loneliness does come up, but I have friends that I call. They're my *companionship boyfriends*. When I'm feeling a little lonely we go to the movies or we go bowling, but that's it and that's where we keep it. I can laugh and have fun with them.

Most people say oh don't cry, but it's ok to cry. Right after I kicked him out, I was just tore up. One of my best girlfriends came over with a bottle of wine. She grabbed two glasses and said, "I'm outside." She poured wine in the two glasses and lit a cigarette. She didn't say one word, she let me sit there and cry about everything. She sat there for over an hour with me. She never tried to offer advice, she just listened. Then that was it. I got up and she said, "Shake it off, let's go. We got to go to work tomorrow."

Sometimes you need somebody who's not going to tell you what to do or instigate stuff. You just need someone to listen, someone to say, "You have a presence here, just let it all out." Scream, cry, do what you've gotta do to get it off your chest. Then keep going.

I also realized I had to change my circle of friends. I had girlfriends I was close to, but they were takers, they were like parasites. They were no better than my husband because they were sucking me dry. They were constantly taking, but they weren't giving back. I started letting people who brought me drama go. If you know more than all your friends in your circle then, you're in the wrong circle. I should be in a circle where I am constantly learning something from the people and they should be learning something from me, too.

This is how I explain my choice to get a divorce. There are five of us, the three kids, my husband and myself. In our life, a hurricane was approaching because the relationship was so jacked up. God told me you need to sacrifice one person and kick them off the raft and the other four will survive. Or you can keep all five of y'all on the raft and go under together. So I kicked my ex's ass off that raft and here we are today, surviving. That's how I look at it.

We had to kick him off the raft, because all five of us couldn't go down with him. The kids and I are thriving, we're on top. My kids are great; they're healthy, smart, respectful, good kids. My ex is drinking and driving and getting DUI's. He's got to get a breath machine put on his car. His license is suspended and he can't keep a job. I look at him and say, "Thank you, Jesus, you knew my purpose. You knew that that was not for me." I have no regrets, because if I hadn't married him, I wouldn't have my son, AJ. I wouldn't have been able to save him from that life. I am most grateful for that alone.

A Real Friend

LISA

If I'm having a bad day or things are stressful, I try to take a minute and ask myself, "What am I stressed about?" All I have to do is read the front page of the paper to know instantly it's not that bad. You don't want to get self-absorbed during this period. That happened to me.

My ex-husband had our son on alternate Thanksgivings. Those years my friends who were divorced or single who had family issues and I would have what I called the *Misfit Thanksgiving*. A lot of times we would go to Florida to celebrate. We'd all gather around this big table. It was this open, joyful Thanksgiving where everybody just got together and hung out.

Late one night I was talking with a group of friends. I was just going on and on about everything that was happening since the divorce in my life. One of my friends who is like a mentor to me stood up and said, "That's it! *Stop it, stop it, stop it*! You are *so* self-absorbed!" I started crying. She told me that she wasn't trying to hurt me. Then she hugged me and said to me, "But just stop it. I can't take it anymore; just get out of your head." She continued to hug me and yell at me at the same time. She told me she wasn't trying to be mean, but she cared about me and somebody needed to tell me. Of course, it was a lot deeper than that, but you get it.

I was kind of mad at her. She was talking to me like that and it made me cry. Then she started crying because she didn't mean to hurt my feelings, but she said I had to hear this. My God, it was like a light bulb came on. It had been close to two years since the breakup. I was still overwhelmed, but I needed to hear that. I am grateful that she helped snap me back.

My Way

CYNTHIA

I am most grateful for my friends. I had put my friendships on the back burner during my marriage. When I was going through this personal crisis, all of them, without exception, stepped up and were simply there. You hate that it takes a tragedy of sorts to help you remember how important and special people are to you. It was great though and I am most thankful for the fact that they were there. They knew I appreciated them being there.

In the beginning of the breakup I was trying to fill time. I began to do the things that I liked to do and wasn't doing when I was married. My friends and I started looking for other opportunities to connect. We went to brunch, museums and concerts at outdoor venues and things. It was almost like being a young adult again, hanging out. We went to a major jazz fest, it was great. There was no worry about, "he doesn't want to go." I didn't have to get approval or clearance to do this or that. I felt a sort of freedom and liberation to manage my schedule my own way.

When I was married the things that I wanted to do always felt like a struggle. For example, we went to his company picnic and it was, so not fun, right? But I did the appearance, made the potato salad and did what a dutiful wife was supposed to do.

I worked for a large company and our unit within this company was having a picnic about three weeks later. I happened to not like my job at the time. My ex was like, "Why are we even going to this thing when you hate this job and you hate these people? You need to get another job." I explained that until I have another job, I need to show up at this thing and play the role. He fussed at me the whole way to the event, "You don't even like these people. Why are we bothering with this? You're trying to find another job. What do you care what they think?"

I was like, "Dude, just shut up and let's go."

We were there all of a half hour and he said, "I'm ready to go." I was like, OK.

The key lesson I learned from that relationship is when someone tells you something about themselves, believe what they tell you. He told me very early on in our relationship that he was shallow and selfish. It didn't match how he was treating me at the time, however, so I brushed it under the rug. At the time, he wasn't shallow and he wasn't selfish. He was interested in the things that I was interested in. He was very giving and would go shopping with me, whatever it was I wanted to do. He was also trying to court me, however, and win me at that point. Once he conquered me, he was free to be whoever he wanted to be. If I could use two words to describe him, even now that we have a decent relationship, I would say that he is shallow and selfish, but he told me that.

I learned a valuable lesson months after the relationship ended. The car insurance was a bill that I paid during our marriage. We had a two year policy and he left shortly after the start of the policy. I continued to pay the bill because I was getting the multi-car discount; this is what I am telling myself, right? Don't make waves, just pay the car insurance. When it was time, I called him to let him know

Gratitude

the insurance was expiring. I was taking his car off the policy and he needed to get insurance on his own.

Weeks later I get a call at 3'oclock in the morning. He's drunk; he's been in a car accident and has totaled his car by wrapping it around a tree. He was livid with me because he realized he didn't have car insurance.

What he said made me sit up in the bed, turn on the light and laugh hysterically. "You have made it perfectly clear that you're not going to take care of me anymore." Wait a minute, wait a minute, now you left me, I didn't leave you! It was my epiphany. That's what he was getting out of the relationship. I was taking care of him. He found somebody he thought would take better care of him than I did. He went to where he thought the grass was greener.

I was like, "Wow, this dude is not for me and I really am better off." Before that you would have been hard pressed to convince me that I was better off without him. Until that point, he could have probably come to me and said I made a horrible mistake, would you reconsider and take me back? I probably would have entertained it, but there was no turning back now. From that point forward, he could have said his life was at stake and only I could save him. I would have told him, "I'm sorry, I'll do my best to help our son manage his grief at the loss of his father, but now there is no time for me and you."

For That Season

VICKI

I was thankful that the marriage ended when it did. It was just going to be a continual waste of my time, energy and youth. I am grateful for the people God put in my life at that time, although I thought I was just making friends.

During one of my job transitions when our marriage was starting to hit rough patches, I had to go to Atlanta to train for six weeks. The trainer was the most unlikely person that I thought I would become friends with. She was full of personality and was very boisterous. She was outspoken, she knew who she was and what she wanted and she wasn't afraid to let people know it. She was very secure in herself. She had a low cut, *loooow* cut 'fro and just the way she walked; it took me forever to figure out what her sexual persuasion was.

At first I was almost afraid of her. We were such polar opposites. I am such a girly-girl and I am looking at this woman, going, and she's training me for six weeks?

This young lady's name was Denice, we called her NeNe. About six months after I completed the training, a full time trainer position became available in my region. NeNe applied for the job and got it. That's when our friendship began.

Gratitude

NeNe was the most unique individual I have ever met. She was from Detroit and she had two siblings, a brother Simon who I am still in love with today and another brother, Russell who is already in heaven. Russell passed away from AIDS, so NeNe, her mother, aunts and cousins were all very active in AIDS charities. NeNe's mother and aunts were part of a quilting group in Detroit. They made a square for the National AIDS quilt in Russell's memory.

NeNe had the best sense of humor. We just clicked. She was the *traveling trainer* throughout our region, so she spent a lot of time on the road. At this point, things were getting progressively worse in my marriage so NeNe gave me a key to her apartment. On the weekends when I didn't have anything to do I could go over to her apartment and chill. NeNe was also making a lot more money than I was. She was on a bonus program and once a year when she would get her bonus, she would just give me a chunk of money, like $300 or $500. 'That's just for you." I couldn't understand what that was about. I thought she was a wonderful friend, but I could never repay her. I didn't see that that was God taking care of me through her.

Once my ex did move out I was still on the base and unable to do anything, NeNe and I would hook up on the weekends. She had a unique circle of friends and they became my friends. There was a young lady who had left California with her kid, escaping an abusive husband. There was another young lady who had come from Florida who was trying to find herself. We were like the four musketeers. There was never a dull moment.

I did more craziness with NeNe in those four years than I had in my entire life. She would say I want to see my mama, so we'd jump in the car and drive to Detroit. When I met her mom the very first time, things were starting to go awry in my marriage. I remember her mother saying to me, "How much money do you have?" I told her I didn't have any money. She said, "Well this is what you need to do…" She was trying to show me how to prepare myself to get out of the marriage, how to be able to take care of myself once it was over. I didn't even know this woman.

NeNe's aunt made a doll for me. I used to keep the doll on my desk at work. One day my friends decided they wanted to play a practical joke. They kidnapped my doll! They involved the whole team. When I arrived at work there was a ransom note for my doll, with clues. They took a picture of the doll and put it on a milk carton! Have you seen this doll? NeNe put me in a world that was completely different than the world I was living in at that time.

When the physical abuse started the other young lady who was a part of our group, already knew it. The spirit was all over her and she could sense it. She started talking to me about what I should do and what I shouldn't do. I never even told her what was going on, I was just covered.

NeNe and I are as different as night and day, but the relationship that I had with her and the reason she came into my life when she did is because she was a vessel God was blessing me through, for so many reasons, filling so many voids, and no questions asked.

I have no communication with any of these people today. If you had asked me at that time in my life if I would ever NOT be in communication with them, I would have told you absolutely not. I'll be talking to them until the day I die. These are my cut buddies for life.

I don't even know if any of them know I have a child. Maybe NeNe knows. My daughter is almost eight years old. I can only say that God put them in my life for a specific season. I didn't even know I needed them. I felt like I needed them because I depended on them so much for support, but I thought that was just my circumstance at the time. Now that I look back I can see God sent just what I needed. If you do the right thing, and have the right heart, God will send it. You won't even know what you're getting at the time, but it will come.

Karma

TERESA

I happen to be an outwardly happy person so people think that life has been easy for me. That is so far from the truth. I believe in life we have a choice in how we react to things. We can choose to be happy.

It doesn't mean that bad things haven't happened, because they certainly have. I lost incredibly dear friends at the Hyatt in Kansas City in 1981 when it crashed to the ground, and hundreds of people were killed. I was there that night and escaped with my life. I lost all my money in the market after the Dot-Com era. That was a big blow because I have to take care of myself. In Katrina, my family lost everything out in the Bayou; that was my family's wealth. It's been one thing after the next.

I knew I couldn't let it define who I was. When I was getting divorced there were many things of my ex's in my possession. In particular, there was a motorcycle. According to the terms of our divorce decree he did not retrieve it in time. It now belonged to me, it was rightfully mine. The court said it was mine and I could have kept it, but I knew the karma that would have come back to me would have been so bad.

That motorcycle meant everything to him. Although he was mean and vindictive toward me, I knew keeping it was the wrong thing to do. I had to give it to him and be gracious about it. I wouldn't let selfishness and pettiness define who I am and that's exactly what keeping it would have done. I have recovered from so much and am grateful for who I am becoming because I am a work in progress.

Forgiven

Dina

I took a spiritual beating when we were divorcing. I really believe in the biblical sense of marriage. I know how the Bible says God hates a divorce. I looked into it from every aspect. I read about it, went to some pastors and talked with them.

The one thing I didn't want to do is disappoint God. My gratitude was learning I could be forgiven. Not only did God forgive me, he was going to pull me through as well. He held me during the time I was going through the process. I was on my knees thanking Him every step of the way.

I understand now why God hates divorce. Even if it's an easy divorce it's still such a hurtful thing, it cuts deep. I prayed to God and said, "Thank you for understanding we're not perfect. I really wanted this to work, and I really thought this was going to be forever. I do believe what you say that marriage should be forever, and I still want that one day. I am sorry it had to go this way." My gratefulness is for the spiritual impact on my life.

Three Things

CAROLINE

My gratitude is to God for seeing me through this, my parents for their enormous support and for my son. Those three things kept me going. I don't know how my son and I would have made it through those times without my parents because my ex was extremely difficult. My prayer life was critical.

Gratitude is something that I feel every day. I give thanks every day, more than once a day because it could have been so much worse.

A Good Steward

TAMRA

Gratitude is a good subject for me because I don't have a lot. I stopped working to stay at home with our son with special needs. After we got divorced, my ex took his salary, and that was all the money we had. I have literally been on welfare and food stamps and all that, so it's really the grace of God that has me here today.

My family gave me a big lump sum of money at one point, which was such a huge blessing. I stretched those funds so they lasted for an entire year. During that time I began to cook all my food. I don't eat out or drink alcohol because I do want to be a good steward of my time and what I have. I could be focusing on not having a lot of money and easily drink too much or eat too much, to deal with my emotions, but then I wouldn't be dealing with my emotions, because I am eating ice cream over them. I make a great effort to face my feelings and deal with my fears and confront my insecurities. It is not easy, but I always get on the other side of it. Over there I look at me as this incredible, dynamic woman that has a lot to offer to the world, my child, my friends and my family. It's been good.

Life and Love

SHEREE

I am grateful for my life. That sums it up. I am grateful the Lord has allowed me to be in a position to love properly. I'm serious about that. I've known folks that struggle with receiving and giving love. I'm not as torn and scattered as I could have been. I am excited I can feel love.

Learning

KIM

My gratefulness is for my family. Now it's just my brother and me. I am very grateful for him because he continues to play a big role in the lives of my sons, both of them. I am grateful for my church family. We are close and they've known us for a long time.

I learned from the struggles. I am grateful for the things I have gone through and where I am now. I might not be rich, but I am better off than I was back then. My Lord and Savior, Jesus Christ has always done it for me. I know he can do it again for someone else.

A Home

KATHY

I thank God everyday that I have a home. My mortgage payments are up-to-date and I work to improve it so I keep my equity up. I am grateful to God for all that I have, especially two physically healthy kids and one of them getting mentally fit. I am also thankful for my parents.

I know God provided the things I have in my life. He's blessed me with it all and it makes me feel really great. I try to teach both my kids if you work at something hard enough you'll get the gratification of enjoying it.

Starting Over

ADRIENNE

I'm remarried and when you build something with someone for 25 years, it includes your financial life. Most times divorced people have less. It could be the man who has less, it could be the woman; it could be both.

My ex and I had a pretty big house, but I was unhappy in it. I thought, so what if the house I have now is a little smaller? I'm much happier in it. Wouldn't it be great if I have a husband in that house that will talk with me? Have great conversations when we travel. We could call each other during the day and share really funny stories.

I sacrificed having what two people built financially together for 25 years to start over and build a life with someone from scratch again. It was worth it.

Independence

Alexis

I was pretty much the head of household from an earning perspective. I am thankful I have the ability to take care of myself. I remained independent enough in my relationship so I didn't experience a sudden void. I am very grateful I managed my relationship in a way that I didn't lose my financial or spiritual wherewithal.

I'm grateful I had the mortgage in my name alone. That was one of his concerns that he wasn't on the mortgage or my checking account. There must have been something in me that said perhaps this wasn't going to last. I kept the mortgage in my name so there were no issues with that. We kept separate finances and I think that that was important, too. Not that we were selfish, but that level of separation of finances allowed me to not have as much concern around freedom and what that meant. I never had to worry too much about, "will I have to stay in this relationship to have something?" Because I didn't have to.

It was a second marriage for me. That may have had something to do with the separation of finances. I'm grateful for learning the first time.

Two Things

MELISSA

Not having a partner was something that was very difficult for me. Most of the men who expressed an interest in me were not men I was interested in. I realized I had to step my game up and become a different kind of person if I wanted to attract a different type of man. That meant I needed to focus on me. So that's what I did each and every day. It was hard and there were days I fell off the wagon, but I dusted my butt off and started again.

There were two experiences that occurred within a year after my divorce that made me grateful I had ended my marriage, but in different ways.

At an industry event, I met a gentleman whose company was doing business with a customer, who the company I work for was also trying to sell services to. We chatted and agreed to meet the next week to discuss how I could secure a meeting with a key decision maker. I went to the restaurant for our meeting and greeted him at the bar. Our meeting began at three thirty so there were very few people in the restaurant. Less than ten minutes after we began talking, he slid the customer contact's business card across the bar to me. I looked at him and said, "Well, thank you very much; I guess this'll be a short meeting."

He offered me a glass of wine. I said, "I don't know, this is kind of a business meeting." The bartender was standing there and obviously this guy has been at this restaurant many times before. The bartender asks, "Can I get you something?" Before I can reply, the gentleman says, "She thinks this is a business meeting, but she doesn't realize that it's really our first date!" Wow, I was speechless. I almost wanted to fall off the bar stool.

That was the start of a wonderful romance. It was totally unexpected and came just when I started to find my groove again. I was just being me, the real authentic me and this fantastic guy found me, spoiled me and loved me. If I never have another romance like that again for the rest of my life, I am glad that I was at the place in my life where I was ready to receive it.

I think if God blessed me in that manner and I'm only this far into perfecting myself, I know I have so many more incredible experiences to come. I know I have to do the right thing, however, and make the right choices. That's where my other story about relationships and gratefulness begins.

I went out on a Friday night alone to listen to some jazz at a place where many of my friends hang out then have a nice dinner in another part of town at a favorite upscale spot. I enjoyed the first set then visited a couple of tables, chatting with friends during the break. As the band gathered to begin the second set, I grabbed my coat and headed for the door. A very attractive man approached as I crossed the room. I had noticed him watching me earlier.

"Leaving so soon?" he asked. We had a casual conversation. He tried to convince me to stay for the next set, but I advised him I was going to my favorite seafood restaurant for dinner. He tried to guess which restaurant; I laughed and advised that he was wrong with every establishment he named. I finally told him the answer, we laughed together and I left the venue.

Gratitude

As I enjoyed the bread basket and a glass of wine that evening at the restaurant, someone stood behind my chair. I turned to see the gentleman from the jazz event. He had followed me twenty miles across town without even knowing my name.

He joined me for dinner, wine and conversation that started with music and current events, drifted to popular culture then veered into light flirting. As dinner came to a close he says the unbelievable. He mentions his wife, casually, like it didn't really matter at all. After he dropped that tidbit of information, the evening ended rather quickly. He walked me to my car and said he understood my position, but he wished I would reconsider. Then he tried to kiss me!

As I drove home I thought about that man's wife waiting for him to return home. I am so grateful living happier after has meant peace and transparency in my life. A life filled with deception, lies and distortions of the truth are not a part of what I have to deal with anymore.

Healthy and Wise

PEGGY

Sadly I have to admit that I'm learning rather late in life to express gratitude. I had nothing for so long that there was a period where all I wanted was more. I wasn't asking anybody to give me anything. I just worked hard to get more.

I found out that no matter how much you have, without your health, none of it means anything. This year I will be a 26-year cancer survivor! When I was diagnosed I was given one year to live, so I am grateful for my life.

I had been divorced for seven years when I was diagnosed. One year away from graduating from undergraduate school. I was getting to the point where I felt like I was going to have a fantastic life. But when I received the diagnosis, I was like "oh, my God, here I've gotten my life together, I can't die."

It took so long for me to get over all the emotional crap I had gone through with my ex-husband. Now I was becoming this educated, grounded, feisty, fun, cute-as-heck woman and I found out I had cancer. I'm not going to complain because it made me who I am today, a God loving woman who is a jazzy old babe on the side.

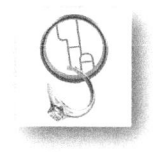

A Positive Spin

JACQUELINE

I am grateful that I was able to manage my thoughts when going through this process. At one point I had a real selfish moment when it was time to sell the marital house after the children were grown. When his attorney sent the offer for my share of the proceeds from the sale of the house, I decided that I had to make sure that I got my *fair share*. After all that my ex had done to raise our children, I decided I wanted what I put into this place.

So sure enough when he sent the paperwork, I looked at it and I said, let me find my receipts. Now let me get my attorney to check this out. Then as the ugliness through the process unfolded, something came over me as I was praying. It said, "Just take it. Just take whatever it is and keep it moving." The money was enough for a down payment on a house in the place where I was living. That was all I wanted, so I agreed. But for a while I was getting a little ugly with it, you know? That was just craziness!

Life is good now. I try to keep a positive spin on things. The way I grew up, sometimes we didn't have heat. Sometimes we didn't have lights, but my godmother always kept that positive spin on everything. I got that from her.

My Children

DANIELLE

My gratefulness is to God for using my children to save me. I was the parent and thought everything I was doing was for them. But I realized that everything they did was for me. My kids actually laid down their lives for me and were the ones who brought me into myself.

My children helped me get happier after because they brought out every important aspect of my character; who I am, and kind of perfected it. Each one of them in their own way affected me in different ways.

My kids had a meeting one evening. They called me into the meeting and said, "You need to leave." They told me, "we've watched this for a long, long time and we've talked about it. If the reason you are staying with him is for us, then you need to leave, because we don't want to be here either."

My children told me it was not their plan to grow up in a house of constant domestic violence, turmoil and chaos. We can't bring our friends home from school, we can't invite anybody over. We can't do anything normal kids do because this house is so crazy.

Gratitude

Then they told me that they wanted me to be real, I asked them to define real. I thought they were too young to understand, the youngest one was eight, the oldest 14 at the time. My son told me, 'This whole relationship with you and dad and our whole existence here is fake. We know that you're not happy, but you fake smile, you fake cook dinner and you fake clean up and do the laundry and stuff. You want everybody to think you're happy and everything is OK, when it's not. We would rather you just be real."

That changed me. I realized they were being perfectly honest with me. No more faking, no more hiding behind anything. My kids wanted me to be real. So I think in an instant I went from being Mary Poppins to Madea!

Chapter Seven

LIVING IN THE MOMENT

Many women in this chapter talk of acknowledging that the small steps they take in moments each day will lead to their overall goals. They are unafraid to admit a mistake, then right themselves and decide to move forward and seek more balance for their lives.

They think positively and listen. And they understand they can't fix everything so they have few regrets.

No Regrets

LISA

I take time to contemplate and reflect 'cause sometimes I'm rolling, rolling, rolling every day. On Sunday, I try not to plan anything. I sit around and think about my week and the things I'm thankful for, but I don't go to church. I'm religious; I just don't go to a place, if that makes sense. For me it's a personal thing, a one-on-one thing. I have my own religion with God in my head. I read and think on my own.

I'm interested in people and what they do. As long as they're good people and they're trying to do the right things, I can be around them. I glean things from their perspective. I'm more of a nonconformist religious person.

I'm a strong person and I try not to think bad thoughts. If somebody acts in such a way to be mean or hurtful, I can be very outspoken. I don't hold things in, I deal with them. I try to live my life and do good things. I try to do the right thing, whatever that is for me. I don't want to regret anything. I try to make decisions and stick with them.

Listen

ALEXIS

I live in the moment, regularly. Living in the moment requires listening. If you're so busy talking that you can't listen, it takes you to another place. I try to be careful to listen to what's not being said, too. Interestingly, when you're used to being alone, you pick up on more of what's unsaid than said. I believe you can be more objective about the motives and feelings that people are sharing. Living in the moment for me is listening to what is not being said.

Therapy

ADRIENNE

I went to therapy. I decided that just because my ex wouldn't go it was no reason for me not to get help getting through this. Initially it was a little intimidating going to therapy to talk about someone who's not there. I started to feel stupid after a while. Why am I talking about this person and he is not even here? I realized that it wasn't about him. It was about me. It was about how I moved forward. I put all my feelings about going to therapy by myself aside and started the process.

I was fortunate to have an exceptional counselor. I thought things had to be just right. I learned that sometimes things just aren't right. Sometimes you don't have to have the last word; you have to live for today and take tomorrow as it comes. Before I went to see her, I didn't think that way.

I stopped worrying so much about the future. I tried to tackle what was in front of me. When you're getting a divorce something happens every day, one day the kids are upset, the next day your estranged spouse is asking "where is this, where is that?" I just stopped worrying and that gave me such freedom. I began to see the future, to see how things could be, once I got past this. I got through the day-to-day and learned to live in the moment by getting the right therapy.

Moment

CYNTHIA

I think the key to being happier after is to simply decide, the same way love is a decision. You have to decide, "I am going to be happy." I'm moving forward from this point. I'm not going to be stuck in this ugly space just because this happened to me.

During those first six weeks or so I got to a point where I was disgusted with myself. I would just cry, cry, cry, cry, cry…I needed to move on. I got sick of me. After that, I think it became a whole lot easier for me to just think, I can do this. It's not the end of the world and life does go on, so just get on with it.

It was hard and it took about a year to get to that place. One thing that helped me a lot was a change of scenery. I moved. When I left the house I shared with my ex, it felt like a new beginning. I didn't just move to a house in the same neighborhood. I moved to an entirely different state. Now geographically it wasn't that far, but it was a new setting. I got a new job not long after that. All the things I felt were on-hold when we were together began to happen. There was movement. It was affirming because I didn't need him for all this positive stuff to happen. It also made me wonder, 'Was he holding me back in some way? Was I so focused on what he wanted that I wasn't doing things that could have moved my situation forward?' Absolutely, I can say without a doubt that that is the truth.

Not Perfect

GRETCHEN

Living in the moment is tough for me because of my concern about financial issues. I'm one of those people with spreadsheets upon spreadsheets upon spreadsheets. I am always planning ahead, so I had a hard time with living in the moment.

I met a person through the leadership group, who had a prayer meeting in their house every Sunday. It included a discussion on the concept of 'live for now,' you know, be in the moment. At the end of the discussion, they would blast music and everyone would start dancing and being joyful all over the house. Being with those people taught me to let go of the little, stupid things in my head that were telling me what I was supposed to be like. I learned to laugh more and I stopped taking myself so seriously. That was hard for me because it's part of my nature. I take what I do seriously, so as a result take myself seriously.

I had to recognize people make mistakes and that's OK. That used to drive me to distraction and sometimes it still does. While it annoys me when people don't do what they're supposed to do, I'm even harder on myself.

I've learned that part of living in the moment means understanding that I'm not perfect. I'm not the savior of the world and I can only do so much. So, if I'm not able to get there, wherever there is, I've got to let go and stop being so hard on myself.

Let No One Disrupt

KIM

I was intimidated and very scared. I didn't know how I was going to manage as a single parent, but everything is a process. I took one day at a time. I shed some tears and asked, "Why did this have to happen to me? What did I do wrong?" But I managed to hold on, doing the best that I could.

I learned to stay focused and not allow anyone or anything to get in the middle of my plan for my children and me, even if I made mistakes along the way. Like the guy that I got involved with who became too comfortable after months of dating him. He said some hurtful things to me and he verbally abused my son.

That's when I stepped in and said, "I'm done." I told my sons, "You don't have to worry about this guy anymore." I had had enough. He said I was weak-minded and he thought I needed a man. I have a home, a car and a job and he was bringing nothing to the table. I became wiser and learned from my mistakes.

Balance Sheet

SHEREE

When my sister died, in my heart I questioned her early and sudden death. I wondered why she entertained an illness that could have been prevented or at least delayed. When we entertain things that don't have to be, we're taking away from something else. All the time that I entertained life with my ex, how he treated me, how he dogged me, how the church treated me, it brought a sense of sickness and illness on the inside of me. I said, "No, no no. I am not going out like that." This is robbing me of time.

I began to replace my thought pattern with positive stuff. It was like a balance sheet. I saw folks being assets and I saw folks being liabilities. At the end of the day, I wanted my balance sheet to balance out. So I had to get rid of the liabilities, the negative thoughts, hurt and the pain. The stuff I'd been carrying around. That's what I did and that's what I do. I replace them with things I know will bring about a sense of satisfaction, love and peace. That's my thing, peace. I mean, you've gotta have peace.

A Little Bit Everyday

Melissa

Living in the moment means that every small step and action I take can lead me to a new and better opportunity. It was the 'how do you eat an elephant concept?' I had to take this journey one bite at a time.

I decided there were some things I wanted to do in my life, or at least try. I was starting a little late, since I was almost 50 when I decided to separate. I thought if I don't try this stuff now, in twenty years I really will be too old! I read a lot of self help books and they always talked about people like Colonel Sanders and Grandma Moses. They didn't start their things with chicken and painting until they were old and they were able to see things through. Why not me?

I started taking classes. I took a storytelling class, screenwriting classes, and dance classes. I did a lot of things to expand my mind, to meet new people interested in the areas that I wanted to do. I don't share my dreams with everyone, but I live in the moment by accomplishing small steps that will eventually lead to fulfilling my big dreams.

I Do What is In Front of Me

TAMRA

Living in the moment has been a big thing for me. When you have a child with disabilities you don't know who they're going to be, at least we didn't. Doctors can't give you that information at the beginning. They can't tell you, they're going to have this, or they're going to have that. The entirety of it is a moment-by-moment experience. That included my husband coming home one day and saying, 'I think it's over.'

At that time we were trying to find out if our son could hear. He did not pass a hearing test for the first time. There were these hearing tests, all of these appointments and things going on with our son's development and then he came home and said he was leaving. I didn't know how it was going to work out, but I said, 'it will work out.'

I just kept doing that thing that was in front of me and I still do. The unknown is all I can guarantee. I have no idea what's next, but I tend to make it through the day and it's been pretty good so far.

Through evictions, cars breaking down, no money, all sorts of stuff, I am still here.

My ex and I celebrate our son's birthday together. Our son, my ex and his girlfriend, my son's grandmother and I all celebrated together this past Christmas. We are kind to one another. I want my son to know we all love him and we're all here for him, to serve him and to make sure he's in a safe, wonderful place. Every day I have to make a choice for that kind of love to occur, every single day. Most days I do.

You're Going to Have It

PEGGY

My music is making me live happy after. I've been singing for over 40 years. I've had both up and down moments. I would never, ever say I don't want to do this again. Even if I came back 29 times after I die, I would always wanna be a singer. Hopefully I would be a more successful singer. God knows I was blessed with a voice. I figured that out quite a few years ago. Even when I thought I didn't have one, people would let me know I did.

During the years when I wasn't making my own decisions, things didn't happen like I thought they should. Back then, I made some decisions that were based on my children.

I had an opportunity one time to go out of the country, but I didn't because I had small kids. They were sending artists to Europe to get good reviews and then they would come back to the states and all of a sudden, they'd be a star. Lots of people did that. So I could have said, "Oh what could have been"…whatever.

Here's the thing. I figured out we do not have control over this. We have to be grateful for every moment because God is the one in control. The fact is that whatever you are supposed have, no matter what you do, if you are supposed to have it and God wants you to have it, you're going to have it. I understand that whatever I am doing now and where ever I end up, it's going to be where God wants me to be. So I enjoy the moments I have.

Not the Avenger

TERESA

I could not live in the moment immediately after the breakup. Men would ask me out and I would abandon them at meals because I thought they were total slime-balls. Or I would find out while I was having dinner with them that they were married. I would stand up and reprimand them in front of everyone and tell them they were despicable people and I would storm out of the restaurant. I could not live in the moment, so I didn't have a fun time. I was self-righteous. These guys were going down. I was the avenging angel.

There are so many men out there that think that I am a total nut-case. It took over a year for me to become a decent person. I finally had to come to grips with myself. I was like, god Teresa, get a grip. I was totally out of control, but I had to go through that. I finally had to say, enough is enough. I don't even like myself. Who wants to be around that; it was painful and ugly.

I went from being the person who accepted everyone to being the person who accepted no one. The pendulum swung for me completely the opposite way. It's not who I am now, but it's who I was.

Living in the Moment

When he cheated on me it made me the victim for everything. Every man was going to pay for it. Every single man was going to pay for what my ex-husband did to me.

Now, I just let things wash over me and enjoy just what's happening in the moment. Granted, it doesn't mean that I have to tolerate the things that are bad, but I can choose to not be around it. I am more cautious about men.

I am closer to getting back to myself as a free spirit of light and not having everything at the same level of intensity. It takes time to deal with it. To me the acknowledgement of it is living in the moment.

No Rentals

CAMILLE

Every moment counts. Life is just not promised. It takes more effort to frown and be angry than to smile. One of my girlfriends and I have a saying, "I will not allow you or the devil to rent space in my head today." If you allow them to rent space in your world then you're frowning and angry like them. When someone pisses you off or they hurt your feelings they're taking up space in your head. They say, "I'm gonna give you a nickel for 50 percent of your brain." You're focused on it, you're thinking about it and you're mad. I use what I call backward psychology, to kill people with kindness.

For example, my ex-husband knows it bothers me when he doesn't show and he's not supportive of our kids. On holidays, our arrangement for the kids was for them to stay Thanksgiving with me and he would have them for Christmas. I asked him if he wanted me to save some of the gifts that I had purchased to be opened at his house on Christmas morning. He said no, I'm good. On Christmas I was out West visiting my sister, so I call my baby and she's crying saying Santa Claus didn't bring her anything! Her dad is in the bedroom asleep with his girlfriend instead of getting up, cooking them breakfast and trying to make it up to them. He says he'll take them to the store later on. Well, it's Christmas day and the stores are closed! Needless to say I was ticked off. I told him, you will never get my kids on Christmas again. You know he's rented *all* the space in my head that day!

This past Christmas he was supposed to get them the day after Christmas. He said I don't know if I'm gonna be able to make it because I don't have money for groceries. In previous years, I gave him money to buy groceries and saved some presents so he could give them to the kids. It was almost like I was still in the relationship, still taking care of his responsibilities. I wasn't doing it anymore. I told him, "You don't have money for groceries? You didn't get them a gift? Well, OK, it's no problem. I have them covered. They got everything on their lists. Whenever you feel like you can come up with gas money and you have time to see them, you know where they live. You have a good day." That's how I handled it. I didn't allow him to rent that space. I went in a completely different direction and he didn't know how to take it.

Sometimes you just have to make people realize they no longer hold that control over you. You can no longer make me angry. You can no longer play with my emotions and string me along. Because that's what they'll keep trying to do once they realize you're out of their grasp. The divorce is over, you're gone and you're living your life. They need some kind of string to pull so they can feel comfortable within themselves. I take it one day at time and I don't allow them to rent space between my ears. That's how I live in the moment.

About You

VICKI

The small steps aren't really small steps. You might think that they're small steps in the beginning, but when you get where you're going, you'll look back and see that it was all part of a bigger plan.

Sometimes you can't say, I'm not in a position to do this. I didn't have a place to stay. I knew I wanted a house, but I wasn't able to buy a one at that time. I had to figure out, how to position myself to make that a reality at some point in the future? It was not a dream, it was a goal. How do I get there?

Well, the first thing I've got to do is get out of debt. What is it going take for me to get out of debt? Do I really want that? Yes, I really want that. You make up in your mind what you want for yourself. You do that after you get to a point where you can focus on yourself, when it becomes about you.

One Minute

CAROLINE

In some ways, I'm an overachiever in my own mind. I can be impatient and want things done, but I have learned from age 30 to now that you really have to take one day at a time. Sometimes you have to take one moment at a time.

When you get up in the morning, you don't know what's going to happen. The only time I count a day complete is when I go to bed at night. I am grateful when I wake up the next morning. I know too many stories of people who woke up in the morning thinking they were going to have a wonderful day and something tragic happens. I say, I take it one minute at a time rather than one day at a time.

Seconds and Frames

KATHY

I live in the moment every second of the day. I take life as it comes. I've been working in television operations for almost 30 years. Most people think of time in hours and minutes. At work, I have to think of time in seconds and frames.

When something happens, whether it's good or bad, it only takes a millisecond for it to occur. If you watch you'll see that things build up to what eventually comes out as a catastrophe or a wonderful thing. Looking at life in that manner has made me enjoy each moment, living it all a second at a time. Every second counts. Tomorrow is not promised. Live life the way it makes you happy.

Do Today

Dina

When you know that you're heading down the long road to divorce, you look at the big picture. You see the finances and all this other stuff you have to take care of by yourself. You see in the grand scheme that this person is going to be gone and you have to take on 100 percent of everything. It seems insurmountable. I found out it's a day-by-day thing.

I trusted in God. In knowing that he will supply, even when you least expect it, in ways that you least expect. Don't look at the bottom line, the big picture of oh, I'm gonna have this house by myself, and I don't know whether I can take care of this rent or this mortgage. Don't look at that. Look at the here and now. What has to be done today? You can become overwhelmed by the bottom line picture. Get through what you need to get through for that day. Worry about tomorrow, tomorrow. That's what I did.

It is overwhelming when you first look at it. 'Oh my gosh! What am I gonna do?' Live in the moment and don't worry about the fact that he's not here and I gotta make that payment next month. Because it's coming and if you can't afford it, worrying ain't gonna help!

You have got to take care of yourself. That's when you have to really step it up. It sounds crazy, but that's the best time to get your nails done, or get a little facial or a makeover. A stress reliever.

Another small step, your support system. Who is gonna be your friend through this? You need them immediately and often. Find out who your core person or persons are, but not too many. They can help you get your head on straight.

When I'm stressed I can't see things clearly. The obvious isn't obvious for me. I have to surround myself with people who can tell me, you need to do this, or ask have you ever thought of calling this person. When I'm super stressed I can't even think of the simplest stuff to do. That's when you gotta have your friends; the ones who have your back, the core people you can talk to. They will help keep you focused on those little steps.

The divorce process will take over your life, your every thought and every action. It consumes you and it's always in the back of your mind. If you can find something to get your mind off it, do it. Join a club. Anything fun and interesting, become part of it. Meet some new friends from outside your marriage. Start a new chapter. You know how the last one ended. Now write a new one.

Chapter Eight

TIME FOR YOURSELF

These women know you've got to take time for yourself so you have energy to help others. Slow Sundays and soothing baths. And more of achieving those big life goals.

They tell us to begin loving you, spoiling you, thinking about yourself and tooting your own horn. Their wisdom reminds each of us of the treasure that we all are inside.

Be the Best Person

CAROLINE

I've always taken time for myself. I think that's the selfish only-child syndrome in me. I knew that if I didn't take some time for me, to keep me rested, I would not be recharged and energized to do the next thing.

You have to look out for yourself. If you are a mess then how are you going to take care of other people? In my case, how was I going to take care of my son, if I was constantly tired? You have to take care of you in order to be the best person you can for yourself and others.

I Know Where I Fit

GRETCHEN

When I got married the first time, I went from my parent's house to my husband's house. Then I divorced and got married again, so I've been divorced twice. I was never alone and on my own until my second divorce.

Moving into that apartment alone in the city was an awakening. I honestly did not know how to be by myself. I didn't know how to rest, because I have always been a highly charged person. If I am not doing something I'm slacking off, so it was hard to just chill. But I recently moved to a house on the river. I am so mesmerized looking at the river and I have learned how to chill.

I'm now at a different level, taking time for myself because I know how to make quiet time. When my kids call me, I am right there. I am their only support system. I am learning to say no, however, because I need time, I'm tired right now so give me the weekend. Let me recharge my batteries and then I can help you. My kids are grown, my daughter is married and in her late thirties. My son is grown and in his early thirties. When they need me though, especially my son, it's "Mom, now!" Nothing has changed since they were in diapers.

Being able to help my children is part of my joy and part of my thankfulness. With God's help I've been able to rebuild myself and regain the things that I lost. Not just the material stuff, but the stuff that's important like my self-esteem. Also looking at my financial future, someday when I retire, I can retire! God has been so kind to me. I find a lot of pleasure in helping my kids and my friends.

When I look at it all, I'm a different person than I was back then. There are some things that are still there, but I think my awareness of who I am in this world has totally changed. I used to think that there was this little world and this big me. Now, I know where fit in this world. There are still bits and pieces of my old personality, because I was pretty driven. Now when I've had enough, however, I stop and I rest. I learned I need to recharge, I need to have a life. So I do.

Learning to Say No

PEGGY

I'm still learning the lesson to take time for myself. I'm learning it a lot quicker now than I used to because I am learning to say no to my adult children. I didn't know how to say, "OK, wait." Some people can let their phone ring or turn off their phone, but I've never done that because I have children. You're going to always be my child no matter what. You're just going to be an adult child, but you'll still be my child. So I can't turn off the phone or unplug the phone or any of that stuff, because you might need me.

I'm learning now because my faith is stronger. I realize that I don't have to solve everything for you because I know God's got you, it ain't my job anymore. I am learning, unfortunately a little late, but I'm learning to say no.

Sundays

ALEXIS

I take time for myself on the weekends, particularly on Sundays because Saturdays are usually for errands. I no longer feel guilty about saying, no I can't get together; I've got things to do for myself. Even going to the spa is an indulgence that I didn't particularly do before, but I really enjoy now.

Baths

LISA

I got into baths. Probably a couple of days a week I just sit in the bathtub. I know it sounds crazy, but my son goes to sleep and I am finished; it's the end of the day. I use all kinds of bath salts and stuff. I have tons of it in my cabinet. It really relaxes me. I really try to focus on taking time.

Back To School

ADRIENNE

I told you I've always worked out and I worked out really hard. My therapist asked me' "What do you do for yourself?"

I said, "I work out."

She replied, "That's good, but that's not what I am talking about. What do you do for you? Do you go to church? Do you participate in social clubs? What do you do? You know, forget about working out, that's different.

I thought about what I wanted to do for me. I decided to go back to school to get a master's degree. When I told my therapist what I was doing she said, "I didn't tell you to go do something that was going to stress you out even more." But it was good for me at the time. It was something I had always wanted to do. I decided when I was married that I wasn't going to do it, but once the decision was up to me and I had nobody to answer to, I decided to go ahead and do it. It was difficult, but it turned out to be a good thing. It's different, but I never said that I wasn't different.

De-Program

KIM

For my downtime, I go in my room and get my music playing. In the morning I pray, meditate and read my Bible to gain strength each day. When I come home in the evening, I have to recharge myself because there's a lot that I endure during the work day. I need 10 to 15 minutes to de-program myself. After extremely rough days I might take a drive to the airport or the park to look at the water. If I have more time I take a mini-vacation to the beach.

That's my downtime, when I relax and think how I am going to get through some other things. I de-program when I read, get into my cooking and when I'm being creative. It keeps my mind on positive stuff instead of focusing on anything negative.

Find the Time to Love You

CAMILLE

That is so important! I cannot tell you how important taking time for yourself is to living happier after. That's where my travel comes in.

I love my kids with all my heart and soul. I would die for them, do anything for them, but we created *mommy time*, for me you know? We already had family time; I made sure I spent time with all of my children, I had three and it was just me. They all have strong personalities, so I made sure they all had a day of the week when we went on a date together. It was just one-on-one time where I could talk with them, interact with them and see how their life was going. I also had my time, *mommy time*. It didn't mean that I always had to get on a plane and travel. It could be something as simple as going to the library, or going in my room and closing the door and being alone, or going for a long ride.

Occasionally, during my commute to work, I ride with no music, just to hear the wheels travel over the pavement. It helps me find my center point, where I can release my stress and everything. Sometimes I just read a book. You have to find time for you, and that's what I do.

Time for Yourself

I also have my own kind of mini-vacations now that my kids are older. I went on a couple of free trips to Atlantic City. Just because I am going doesn't mean I have to gamble. Maybe once per month I go with my laptop and hang out in the hotel room. Get some food and beverages and have a great time. If I feel like going to gamble a little bit, I gamble. If not, I'll go and catch a show.

I learned to do things by myself. I think that when God sends me my husband, (because I'm not looking for him) I'll be ready for him. I can stand on my own two feet. I am not needy. I don't need for him to do everything with me and I don't need for him to take care of me. I want to be able to complement my man. I don't want him to come in and tower over my life. I worked really hard to get where I'm at and I want someone that I can share it with, not take away from it.

So that's what I do. I've learned to do things alone. I can go to happy hour and talk and network. I can travel and go on tours by myself and not feel self conscious or feel like I'm the smallest person in the room because I'm standing there by myself. No, I'll sit right down at the dinner table, even if it's a banquet and run my mouth and talk to everybody.

It's about finding your comfort zone and being able to love you again. Not being vain, but as long as I love me, I don't have to worry or work so hard to get a man to love me. If you're going to love me, you're going to love me for exactly who I am.

Taking the Time to Think

MELISSA

Taking time for me was something I did not do well during my marriage. It may have been one of the contributing factors toward its demise. I was too focused on everyone else and everything else and my dreams and my priorities. My current projects and goals were always on my list of things to do. I rarely have a time when, even when I'm chilling that I can say, everything I want to get done is done. I didn't understand the importance of recharging my own battery and how critical it was to my happiness. Now I do.

It's funny, but I used to take time for myself a lot when I was single and during the first ten years of our relationship. Something shifted and I'm not sure what it was. Whatever it was, however, the result was unhealthy for me.

Now I take time for myself by doing the things I need to do that give me sanity. I walk every morning both for exercise and to clear my mind. I have become laser focused on my creative goals. I'm also working very hard to control negative self talk by giving myself the internal *atta boy* and having gratitude for what I do and for the gifts that I've been given. As I find my way through middle age (yikes, is 50 still middle aged?) I'm taking the time to think more about what my legacy is going to be. I have two children that I love dearly and I know they will be my biggest legacy. I'm very proud of the man that my oldest son has turned out to be. My youngest is finding his way, too. He has a few more years with mom, and I pray I'm able to finish raising him up the right way.

I have learned to toot my own horn, to myself. Not to say it to anybody else, but to internalize the fact that I'm pretty good. I'm a pretty good person. My parents did a pretty good job raising me. I'm a great friend and a great mom. I could be better, but I'm special and I'm loved. I acknowledge all the little things that make up my character and I continue to just love on me. That's what time for myself means to me.

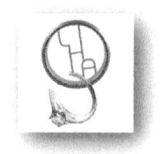

What a Treasure

CYNTHIA

I started some self care things that I hadn't done before. Getting *mani's* and *pedi's*, and little things like that. I asked myself, why weren't you doing this before? I look back on some of the things I started doing after the breakup and I thought to myself why didn't you start going without him? If he was being *pissy* and didn't want to go with you, what stopped you from just going?

If he wanted to do something and I didn't want to go, it didn't stop him from going. I let him upset my little applecart in that way, and so if he didn't want to go to some event then I stayed home. If he was sulking, I would try to smooth it over and make everything fine. I don't want to make it seem like he's as much of an asshole as its sounding like, he's not necessarily a bad guy. He is selfish, but he told me so.

The book club is something that I did for me. I didn't take my son with me and I wasn't accountable to anybody during that time. I really did hold that as sacred. We met once a month and I was there, once a month. That was me time. I was doing what I wanted to do, not what someone else wanted to do.

Time for Yourself

I'd tell any young woman coming up not to sacrifice who you are and what your needs are for the sake of a relationship. It doesn't make any sense to me now.

If he hadn't just up and left, I probably would have been with him for a long time, unhappily. It would have been bearable because we would have been doing things that were productive, he would have been achieving his dreams, our kid would have been great, all of that. If you had seen us from the outside looking in you would have thought we were this up-and-coming dynamic young couple. It's crazy! You get to a point; however, where after giving yourself away, you've forgotten what a treasure you were to begin with. You completely lose yourself.

Precious

KATHY

I have to make time for me. I have all these other things like taking care of my parents and going to visit my son. Whenever my daughter needs me I am on the road to see her. I am always thinking about somebody else. Oh, and I work two jobs! So time for me is almost like an artifact. It's something that I need to work on.

When I do get a chance, I like being here in my house alone. It is peaceful and totally quiet, unless I want to make some noise! And I do, if I want to. If I want to run around the house butt naked I can. It's precious to me, being by myself.

Peace

SHEREE

That's a hard one. The life I live is one of constantly giving. I had to learn how to give Sheree some rewards. I'm still working on that, not to give myself the leftovers because when I get time for myself, it's leftover. I make good use of it when I get a moment, I really do!

It goes back to having peace. I'm OK ripping and running and playing the role of two parents. I'm OK making sure that everybody else is OK. And I'm OK with it because I get it done. I feel gratitude, when I see my child graduating from college cum laude or another earning a law degree. So time for me, there's not a lot of it, but when I get it I make good use of it. I really do. I've just got to find it!

Don't Waste It

VICKI

Your ex has gone on with what they want to do. They may not be accomplishing their goals, and they might be miserable too, but this is the choice that's been made. You need to take care of yourself because they're not thinking about you anymore and they're going to take care of themselves.

We get one life so why would you waste it with someone who either doesn't want you or who doesn't treat you right? They might love you all night long, but if they're not going to treat you right—love and honor, respect and cherish you—well, I can have the crap all by myself. I can inflict all kinds of drama on me; I don't need someone else to do it. You get this one time to go around, you better make it worth your while!

Chapter Nine

The Survey

The survey was launched December 30, 2011 on SurveyGizmo.com. A total of 102 divorced women responded to the survey. The results reported in this chapter are of the 34 women who self reported that they are:

- Living happier after their divorce
- Using the principles of positive psychology to get happier

Question 1: Since the divorce do you consider yourself

VALUE	PERCENTAGE
More Happy	100%
Less Happy	0%
About the Same Level of Happiness	0%

Question 2: If you are happier, please indicate which activities contributed to your increased happiness

Activity	Did Not Contribute	Slightly Influenced	Made a Difference	Contributed a Lot
Looking at Life Positively	3.2%	3.2%	32.3%	61.3%
Pursuing Your Own Self Fulfillment	6.3%	3.1%	34.4%	56.2%
Taking Time for Yourself	6.5%	6.5%	29.0%	58.0%
Practicing Gratitude	6.7%	6.7%	53.3%	33.3%
Knowing That Tomorrow Will Be Better	6.5%	9.7%	29.0%	54.8%
Doing Good for Someone Else	9.7%	12.9%	41.9%	35.5%
Nurturing Relationships with Family	9.4%	15.6%	25.0%	50.0%
Nurturing Relationships with Friends	6.3%	18.8%	21.9%	53.0%
Spiritual or Meditation	13.3%	16.7%	20.0%	50.0%
Practicing Forgiveness	22.6%	12.9%	35.5%	29.0%
Not Taking Everything Personally	19.4%	19.4%	32.2%	29.0%
Shopping (Retail Therapy)	50.0%	20.0%	16.7%	13.3%
Exercising Regularly	27.6%	20.7%	17.2%	34.5%
Dating or Being in a New Relationship	30.0%	26.7%	23.3%	20.0%
Volunteering	44.8%	20.7%	20.7%	13.8%
Counseling/Therapy	50.0%	18.8%	9.4%	21.8%
Getting Remarried	73.3%	3.3%	6.7%	16.7%
Taking Courses/Going Back to School	60.0%	16.7%	10.0%	13.3%
Losing Weight	60.0%	16.7%	13.3%	10.0%
Getting a Makeover	74.1%	9.7%	9.7%	6.5%
Getting Revenge	93.3%	6.7%	0.0%	0.0%

Question 3: Please describe how these activities or others not listed above, helped you feel happier after.

- Allowed me to "exhale" and rediscover my true self and what I am most passionate about.
- Encouragement/support from my immediate family.
- I focused on self improvement and loving myself.
- I walk an hour a day, to open my mind.
- Peace of mind played a major factor in becoming the person I am today.
- The activity took me from the constant bad feelings about myself and my ex husband...it helped refocus.
- Focusing on other things keeps your mind off the emotional loss.
- I felt more self-fulfilled.
- I learned to love myself for who I am and I stopped trying to make others happy at my own expense.
- Focusing on myself gave me the tools to become balanced and healthy so that I could understand and forgive my ex-husband.
- When I was married, my husband took care of everything as far as making sure bills get paid, fixing things, etc. During the separation, I was scared that I wouldn't know how to do anything on my own. But I just kept telling myself that I was smart enough to figure it out and sure enough, I did! I am *so* glad for my independence and it has made me a stronger person, knowing I can live life without relying on someone else.
- They helped me keep my mind on other positive things, so I would not focus on the divorce so much and stay depressed.
- Going to therapy and understanding more about myself and why I felt the need to take on others burdens. In addition to

knowing that I could make it on my own and find my own happiness in life.
- The tension between how I envisioned my life and reality disappeared. I became the sole architect of my life's direction. As a woman, I tend to be inclusive and felt the need to incorporate my spouse's goals. But they never concretely materialized and I found I needed to make my own way and do it with my own voice.
- I think once you accept that it is time to move on, no matter what the reason is for a failed marriage it allows you to grow as a person. Forgiveness was a huge part of this for me. Being angry takes so much energy out of you and serves no purpose other than making yourself miserable while others move on with their life.
- Getting happier was all about taking care of myself and treating me with the dignity and respect I deserved. I lost myself in my marriage and I accepted disrespectful treatment from my husband.
- They made me happier because I shifted the focus off of HIM and put it on myself. I no longer had to walk around wondering what incident or comment was going to irritate me today; I could take each moment as it came, and that bought a tremendous amount of peace and relaxation to my life.
- Don't need much space to say, "I took back control of my life...mistakes and all, and that instantly made me happier even when I made mistakes!"
- I met my ex when I was 28, married him at 31 and we separated when I was 46; 5 years later we finally were divorced. After the separation and divorce, I beat myself over the head thinking that I wasted my life. Yes, I was angry, then I was depressed and then I yo-yoed between angry and depressed. Thank God for girl friends who helped me find myself again.

The Survey

And I thank God for being with me through the whole journey. With my friends and my new relationship with God, I slowly learned how to be alone and truly enjoy the time to be with myself. I learned to experience new things like traveling to a different country by myself – the thought of that initially freaked me out. Exercise and yoga helped me care for my mind and body with the added bonus of dropping a bunch of weight. It took me about 3 to 5 years to find my stride again and each day I thank God for all the blessings he has afforded me.

- Just not having to get permission from anyone to be able to do what I want within reason makes me a happier person. Taking control of my life and not having to cater to someone who is unappreciative for everything you did for them. Getting free from being taken for granted and getting no emotional support from the needy person makes me a much, much happier person. I could go on but that's about the jist of it. Freedom!
- I became more comfortable with and embraced the new, "me". New environment, new mindset, and a new level of love (for myself and others).
- Whether exercise or doing something you love keeps you busy and positive, staying involved helps with not getting stuck in sadness. Realizing that life is what you make it and there's no specific definition for my happiness except what I want it to be. Forgiveness is a beautiful thing.
- Each activity was related to a different phase of the divorce process. The counseling help to pull back the veil of denial and put the situation in a realistic perspective. Once that happened I could then begin to focus on me and look toward the future. I already had robust relationships with family and some friends so my focus was on managing the relationships of the shared friends of mine and my husband.

Eventually that all sifted out and I retained only one or two relationships with friends that he brought to the marriage. It's funny, revenge nor forgiveness were ever a thought! :-) I was already in great shape physically so that just continued. I did however have to live through a phase of financial hardship so there was no retail therapy, but I was ok, with that too, because I knew in order for me to establish my own positive identity I had to clean up the mess. What was waiting on the other side of that was to my over all future benefit and happiness, so I viewed that hardship as a necessary season. I took great pride in doing what had to be done and getting it done.

Question 4: What type of relationship do you have with your ex-husband today? (Respondents can select as many answers as applicable.)

VALUE	PERCENTAGE
I still hate him	2.9%
I have no interaction with him	47.1%
I can be in the same room with him	17.6%
We co-parent our children	20.6%
We are cordial	32.4%
We are friends	17.6%
I am still in love with him	2.9%
We have had sex since the divorce	0.0%

Question 5: If you could do things over would you

VALUE	PERCENTAGE
Get divorced	94.1%
Try to make the relationship work	5.9%

Question 6: If you worked during the marriage did you earn more money annually than your spouse?

VALUE	PERCENTAGE
Not applicable	8.8%
Yes	64.7%
No	26.5%

Question 7: What was your 'aha' moment when you knew you had to end the marriage?

- My life was not getting better.
- Refusal to seek marriage counseling from ex-spouse.
- There was no specific moment but there were multiple signs, which I ignored for several years.
- There were many, but high among them was my ex's disdain for my spirituality.
- When I finally realized I wasn't powerless over the abuse and had choices.
- When I realized he did not want to serve God.
- When I realized he was *unable* to change.
- When I realized that I had to break some "generational" patterns.
- When he said I don't care about whether you're happy.

- When he turned to drug use.
- When my children told me I needed to leave.
- When, gambling became more important to him than formula for our baby.
- Abuse.
- His cheating…and his constant lying.
- When he kicked my ass.
- When weapons and threat entered into the relationship.
- My ex-husband took me on a vacation for my 50th birthday. I knew it wasn't a good idea in my heart but I felt maybe, just maybe if we went it would be ok. It was a nightmare from the start. We didn't have a good time and it seemed like whatever I did or said was wrong. It was *the* worst vacation of my life. I knew during that week that we would never make it and that ultimately we would end our marriage.
- When the "ugliness" directed toward me for all those years started being directed at the children.
- I should have known from the beginning when I preferred to live together rather than get married. But we both had children from different marriages and it seemed like the right thing to do; after all we lived together for 3 years and I didn't want to break the bond the kids had already developed. But, once I committed, I'm one of those people who will give it my all which I did and so I did. The more I did, the less he did. What's that about? But, I think the one thing that made me realize this is not what I want were the lies . . . little white stupid lies in the beginning which should have been meaningless. But to me, those little white lies slowly eroded the trust and respect I had for him. My first aha moment was 5 years into the marriage. Why did I stay – simple, the kids.

The Survey

- When he TALKED AT me for over an hour telling me what he wanted out of the relationship and having NO INTEREST in what I wanted out of the marriage.
- I knew it was time to end things when he repeatedly did things that he KNEW annoyed, bothered and angered me. Not out of necessity or "no other choice" but CHOOSING to do things that he knew would ultimately create friction in our home. I couldn't live like that anymore.
- My 'aha' moment came when I realized I was playing out my wounding with my father in leading our marriage. The negative projections I had of my husband were actually my father's imprint upon me.
- When everything around me was spiraling downward and I knew that I could have two happy people (my daughter and myself). I knew that my upbringing was not mirroring the life I was living.
- When I realized my "ex" didn't want to be the kind of parent I thought he would have been to our son. When I realized he was not a very nice person and could be quite mean which scared me.
- I had been feeling like the marriage was lacking the love that it should have and been trying to rekindle something. But one day he got me a card for our anniversary that read something along the lines of "You mean so much to me. I love you so much. I can't imagine my life without you." The feeling was not mutual at all and I knew that I had to get out, if only so he could be rid of me and perhaps find someone that would return those sentiments.
- I knew in my heart long before it ever happened and I think he did too because he said to me once that I would never leave him as long as my mother was alive. He was right. I had been asking myself daily, "is this all I have to look forward

to for the rest of my life?" Divorce was/is common in my family and I was determined not to join the statistic. As time passed the passive aggressive mental and emotional abuse took a turn to add physical, that's when he decided to leave.
- The moment I found out he was having multiple affairs...we had only been married for 15 months when I learned of just three of the affairs. I threw him out of my home.
- When I realized that he was not going to change or get the help he needed for a drug addiction. I can do bad all by myself rather have someone else take me down. I realized you can't control anyone but yourself and that I am worth more by myself than with him.
- When our social circles spiraled in very different directions and we spent very few hours together simply communicating about our daily goals and accomplishments.
- When I prayed for God to give me a sign that this marriage was over, and within minutes my answer was there.
- When I realized my ex-husband was not willing to work on himself and our relationship. He was not willing to get help for his abusive nature brought forth by low self esteem and alcohol/substance abuse. I never wanted our son to see him verbally and physically abuse me and my gut told me it was a sad way to spend your life.
- I was growing and he wasn't. He also tried to pursue a dream that failed and it was difficult for the family.
- When we went to marriage counseling. That was the straw that broke the camel's back. He did not want to listen and was always blaming everything and everyone else. Not taking constructive criticism and always distorting the issues. Blaming the world for his misery.
- After years of abuse, one particular day, I saw a set of cast iron pots and pans and decided to purchase them. Once the set was in the house, I knew I had to leave before a felony would be committed.

The Survey

Question 8: What was your 'aha' moment when you knew you would be happier after the divorce?

- Enjoying life.
- I knew all along.
- For the first time in months I slept soundly through the night when we agreed on the date he would move out!
- Not sure I would be happier, but I knew anything was better than how I was living.
- Our conversations were nothing.
- Release of control from others saying for me to stay for the sake of the child(ren).
- Seeing the smiles on my children's faces accompanied by the constant laughter.
- The father realization. I took responsibility for my part in our relationship. I stopped blaming.
- There is nothing better than peace of mind.
- When he turned to drug use.
- When I left the home we shared and lived in my own apartment.
- When I noticed my children were at ease and the purchase of my own home.
- When I realized that I hadn't "lost" anything, but had gained everything.
- When I returned to school and I realized my personal worth was the investment in me.
- When he left and my child and I had such peace. No more fights!
- When my dog didn't even notice his absence.
- When my mother called me 30 days after we separated and asked me how I was really feeling.
- When I no longer felt alone. I felt more alone with my ex-husband than I do without him.
- When I realized that after 17 years of marriage that life didn't begin and end with him.

- When I saw the blood.
- When I was safe.
- When the safe feelings finally returned for me and my sons!
- I knew that not being married to him would make me a happier person. Not living with him, not seeing him would bring me peace.
- When I realized I'd never have to deal with THESE particular issues again. I had made a mistake marrying him, and that caused me a tremendous amount of grief, pain and anger. The only thing to do to regain any semblance of the happiness I'd had before was to get divorced.
- When the counselor asked me why I would want to be with someone who didn't want to be with me! Like a dislocated shoulder popping back into place, that put it all in perspective for me. That was the turning point for acceptance and moving forward.
- That took a long time. It took months of therapy, crying, talking with friends, being angry, blah, blah, blah. For at least a year I dated a few men and I was dreadful to them....'I wasn't fit for human consumption!' I needed time! Finally, once I made peace with myself and I forgave myself for being in love with and mourning the loss of what I wanted not what I had....I experienced a slow but eventual 'aha' moment. It took a year and a half....it was not easy but it was necessary. Now...2 years to the day of throwing him out....I am happy again!
- Once the divorce was in progress, I knew that it was only a matter of time before I'd truly be on my own and living my own life.
- When I learned that I was wasting my time with anger and self loathing. I realized how short life was and I found a path through 4 years of one on one counseling and Al-Anon group sessions.

- When I realized that I am a smart, funny, attractive woman who is smart and able to accomplish all my dreams.
- Once I was able to say to one person that my ex and I had separated and they didn't make a judgment.
- That took awhile. It wasn't that I was happy being married but I liked coming home to someone being there. I think when I finally learned how to be alone and truly enjoy that time by myself was also the 'aha' moment when I knew there is great happiness after divorce.

Question 9: What advice would you give to other divorced women who want to live happier lives?

- Concentrate on yourself and your kids, not someone who sucks the life out of you.
- Don't be afraid to love and trust again.
- Don't be bitter, love life and stay positive because it prolongs life.
- Focus on your present and your future, NOT your past.
- Go somewhere, do something, create a life that's tailor-made for you.
- Keep busy, serve Jehovah God to the best of your ability.
- Life will get better. Making changes can be scary but good.
- Love yourself and your child(ren); let go of the past
- Pray and talk to God about any decisions you are about to make.
- Seek God, seek peace, and seek the love within.
- Take responsibility. Don't be a victim.
- Take the time to get to know YOU before getting into another relationship.
- Take the time to grieve and heal before you entangle yourself with someone else.
- Love yourself more than anyone else will.

- If your spouse doesn't love you the way you need to be loved, move on. Love yourself. You only have so many years to do you.
- Please find a way through therapy and self help groups to discover that you are wonderful. Learn to love yourself for all of your faults and good qualities so you can see life with a new positive view.
- Think through all of aspects of your life, decide what you are willing to compromise on and what is non-negotiable, put it on paper and if the non-negotiable things outweigh the compromises, then move on. Keep your good memories and let them reinforce that you can have more without the weight of a bad marriage.
- Journal, read, talk to friends, family, therapists....get angry with yourself, your ex-husband....then start forgiving yourself. Decide what you want your life to look like and work towards that...it may be baby steps forward one day and giant falls backward the next. Start again. Take deep breaths. If your husband was disrespectful of you in any way, imagine what your life would look like in 5 years with that type of behavior. Happiness is a choice....and, it takes a lot of work and it's worth it.
- After the divorce is finished don't dwell on it. Reflect on what you learned in the storm, grow and move on.
- As harsh as this may sound, keep in mind that no one will be willing to change places with you in your casket when you die, so don't surrender your life to anyone other than Jesus Christ while you're alive!
- Focus on yourself and your self worth...Heal before jumping into another relationship. And realize that you don't need a man to prove your existence in this world.
- Become your own priority. Get to the point where a man, future companion or spouse are gravy in your life. The woman should be a whole person, a feast all by herself. That new

The Survey

man, if she chooses to have and receive one should be a compliment, just gravy!
- Please don't rush into another relationship thinking a man can solve your woes. Look for peace and happiness within yourself. Give yourself a chance to recover so that when you do meet the right person he will simply enhance your life but won't be the reason for your happiness. Your happiness should come from within.
- Don't underestimate who you are and don't allow your current circumstances to define who you are or who you can be.
- Enjoy and embrace your independence and know that you are not one of those women who stay in marriages (and miserable!) for convenience. You DO NOT need someone to take care of you and it feels so much better to do everything for yourself. VERY empowering.
- Do what is best for you and your family. People will have an opinion, but at the end of the day you need to focus on what you can live with or live without.
- Get in touch with reality, become involved in a good support group, cherish friends and family - find a place to focus the new energy you will find.
- It's behind you. Let go of any anger you have, and use your marriage as a source of funny stories at your ex's expense, like I do.
- What advice would I give to other divorced women who want to live happier lives? Hmm...I guess I would say that in order to be truly happy, you have to be happy within yourself. No one can make you happy, they can add happiness to your life but they are not responsible for our happiness. That happiness has to come from ourselves. But I would give this same advice to anyone who wants to live a happier life.
- We all leave this world alone. If someone makes the journey easier, brighter, more alive for you, then those are the angels

you need in your circle. Listen and hear what your inner voice is signaling. Trust in yourself and your choices.
- Don't be afraid to take that first step, especially if you are in an abusive relationship, it doesn't get better over time.

Questions 10 and 11: Omitted due to personal data

Question 12: Please indicate your current age

Value	Percentage
Less than 40 years old	6.1%
40-44 years old	6.1%
45-49 years old	15.2%
50-54 years old	33.3%
55-59 years old	24.2%
60-64 years old	0.1%
65-69 years old	3.0%

Question 13: Please indicate your ex-husband's current age

Value	Percentage
Less than 40 years old	8.8%
40-44 years old	2.9%
45-49 years old	17.6%
50-54 years old	14.7%
55-59 years old	29.5%
60-64 years old	8.8%
65-69 years old	11.8%
70-74 years old	5.9%

The Survey

Question 14: Where do you live?
All respondents live in the USA

Question 15: What is your race/ethnicity?

Value	Percentage
American Indian or Alaska Native	6.1%
Asian	3.0%
Black or African American	69.7%
White	24.2%
Native Hawaiian or Other Pacific Islander	0.0%
Hispanic or Spanish Origin	0.0%
Not Hispanic or Latino or Spanish Origin	0.0%

Question 16: What is your ex-husband's race/ethnicity?

Value	Percentage
American Indian or Alaska Native	0.0%
Asian	0.0%
Black or African American	68.7%
White	31.3%
Native Hawaiian or Other Pacific Islander	0.0%
Hispanic or Spanish Origin	0.0%
Not Hispanic or Latino or Spanish Origin	0.0%

Question 17: How long were you married?

Value	Percentage
Less than 10 years	43.8%
10-14 years	25.0%
15-19 years	25.0%
20-24 years	3.1%
25-20 years	3.1%

Question 18: Did you file for divorce?

Value	Percentage
Yes	79.4%
No	20.6%

Question 19: How many years have you been divorced?

Value	Percentage
Less than 2 years	17.6%
2-4 years	14.7%
5-9 years	14.7%
10-14 years	26.6%
15-19 years	8.8%
20-24 years	8.8%
25+ years	8.8%

Acknowledgements

There is no way I can thank all of the people who supported and uplifted me during the process to develop, research and write this book. But there are some people who were instrumental in developing the book you now hold in your hands (or uploaded to your e-reader).

First, to my father and mother, George and Idabel Jones, you are the best parents ever and I love you and thank you for everything. There is no way I can ever repay you for what you have done for me. I hope you are proud of me.

To my siblings, George M. Jones, Jr., Michael G. Jones, Rosalind T. Harris, Lynwood N. Jones, Lydia N. Cole and Audrey E.J. Corley – always believing in all my dreams and assuring me that you all always have my back. I love y'all more than you know.

To my sisters-in-law, Vanessa and Jackie, and brothers-in-law, Michael, Reggie and Hayward, nieces, nephews and cousins, thanks for being my 'fam'; you know I love you always.

My girlfriend, Melody Patrick is a huge part of the reason this book was actually written. You held me down when I thought I was about to fly away on the fears and insecurities hidden within my thoughts. I wish every woman with dreams had a friend like you.

To my first BFF, Cheryl Fernanders, we were born eleven days apart and I hope we live to be 100 together. Thank you for always believing in my dreams.

Thank you to Rev. Sonja Flye Oliver, my pastor and my friend. You prayed for me and this project and preached about living your dreams so many times, I had to believe! I am so grateful to have you in my life.

To Sophfronia Scott, 'The Book Sistah,' my online and telephone seminar writing mentor for so many years. Your "Writing and Publishing Books That Change Lives" seminar in October, 2011 set this project in motion. I will always be your fan.

Thank you to Katharine Sands, Penny Sansevieri and Gina Panettieri for taking time to give me valuable feedback during the writing conference. Professionals like you who give time and consideration to aspiring authors like me should have a special place in heaven. And to Pam Slim whom I also met that conference, your message is inspiring and your generosity of spirit and time during your monthly Q&A calls helped me so much as I developed this to fruition. And not to forget, thanks to Shannon McCaffrey, the survey guru.

To Sara J. Roney of Sunrise Studios (www.SunriseStudiosOnline.com) who designed my graphics for the book cover. Your work is amazing! I can't wait to work with you again.

Thanks to my sister, Audrey E.J. Corley, who used her 30+ years of experience to help me develop the online survey. You are so good at what you do!

Thank you to my editors, my sister, Lydia N. Cole and D. Michael Whelan. You both helped to make this book better. I appreciate your efforts.

Thank you to my brother-in-law, Michael B. Harris for the author photographs. As always, your work makes me smile at myself.

To Dr. Audrey Chapman whose Saturday morning relationship talk show on WHUR-FM radio (and now at whur.com and on Sirius,

Acknowledgements

too) was a godsend for me during my break up. I feel blessed and highly favored to have your foreword as a part of this book.

To Thelma Barker, Willie Jolley, Louis Ross, Ahmad Hassan, Louise Babirak, Monique Sheppard, Carl Carrington, Dwain 'Billy' Southern, Nadia Conyers and Kevin & Cryillene 'Cece' Clark, I appreciate you and your support each and every day.

To all my friends from JWC Bandits, DMV Kickballers, Guns and Roses and all the other teams in the Goombay Recess Co-ed and Women's Kickball Leagues – you helped me release that stress and made me laugh when I needed it. I Love KICKBALL!

Thanks to all the women who took the survey. And a *huge* thanks to all the women who participated in a telephone interview. You rock for me!

Thanks to four people who mean the world to me: OWK, ZCKK, KRKJ and KMK. I list you by your initials but I love you full-out!

To my ex-husband, thank you for the good times.

And last but certainly not least, thanks to God.

Visit the website and join the community at www.LivingHappierAfter.com.

Made in the USA
Middletown, DE
22 October 2020